AMBASSADORS OF ARMSTRONGISM

*An Analysis of the History and Teachings of
The Worldwide Church of God*

by

Paul N. Benware

CHRISTIAN LITERATURE CRUSADE
Fort Washington, Pennsylvania 19034

CHRISTIAN LITERATURE CRUSADE
Fort Washington, Pennsylvania 19034

CANADA
Box 189, Elgin, Ontario KOG 1EO

GREAT BRITAIN
51 The Dean, Alresford, Hants., SO24 9BJ

AUSTRALIA
P. O. Box 91, Pennant Hills, N.S.W. 2120

NEW ZEALAND
512 Dominion Road, Auckland 3

PRINTED IN THE UNITED STATES OF AMERICA

Contents

Author

Paul N. Benware is Professor of Bible and Theology at the Moody Bible Institute of Chicago. He received his B.A. degree from the Los Angeles Baptist College; Th.M. from Dallas Theological Seminary; and the Th.D. degree from Grace Theological Seminary.

Dr. Benware and his wife Anne have four children: David, Laurie, Matthew and Timothy. Dr. Benware's interest in Armstrongism goes back to the days when he lived in Pasadena, California, the center of the Armstrong empire.

Dedication

To Anne, my companion in the ministry of God's truth.

Introduction

Throughout its history, the Church of Jesus Christ has been forced to deal with doctrinal error. The apostles themselves had to deal with individuals who introduced false teachings regarding the law, the person of Christ, the resurrection, sanctification, justification, as well as other important areas of theology, but the refutations and explanations by the apostles did not permanently settle the problem of doctrinal deviation for the church. Since then the orthodox church has had to constantly contend with individuals and groups who have left the basic truths of the Word of God to promote their error.

Today orthodox Christianity is being confronted with an intensification in the propagation of erroneous doctrine. Within the last century many new cults and splinter groups have emerged and grown at tremendous rates. At the present time one of the fastest growing cults in the world is the Worldwide Church of God of Herbert W. Armstrong.

The Importance of the Study
The Claims of the Worldwide Church of God

Herbert Armstrong and his Worldwide Church of God have opened an attack on the foundations of the orthodox Christian Church by denying that it and its teachings are of God. This denial is coupled with the claim that the Worldwide Church of God is the only legitimate channel of God's Word and work in the world today.

And there is only ONE Church on earth today which *understands* and is PROCLAIMING that *exact order of events,* doing the

> WORK of God in preaching His message to the world as a last witness, really "feeding" the true flock. . . .[1]

After discussing the name "Church of God" it is the conclusion of Armstrongite, Herman L. Hoeh, that all other churches and groups are counterfeit.

> These verses prove the NAME of the true Church. Denominations *not* bearing this name could *not* be God's true church. And of all the churches that do bear the name, *only one* could be the *true* Church of God—that one which OBEYS ALL the commandments of God and maintains the FAITH delivered once for all time—the one which *grows* in truth. All others are counterfeit even though they may have the knowledge about the NAME of God's Church.[2]

In reference to their message, the claim is repeated throughout their literature that they alone know and preach the true gospel.

> What is the one and *only* gospel of Jesus Christ? THE WORLD DOES NOT KNOW! It has not been preached for 18½ centuries, strange as that may seem.[3]

Such a claim obviously excludes all churches and denominations today, as well as every individual and movement throughout all of church history. Concerning himself and his followers, Herbert Armstrong declares,

> The prophecies and mysteries of God, sealed *until now*, are today REVEALED to those whom God has chosen to carry His last Message to the world as a witness . . . Christ has opened these mysteries to His servants.[4]

It is important that these claims of exclusiveness be analyzed since they reflect on the validity and credibility of orthodox Christianity.

The Growth and Influence of the Worldwide Church of God

The Worldwide Church of God began in 1934 as a very small and insignificant work, but since then it has mushroomed in size, power, wealth and outreach, until now millions weekly are being influenced by its message. This rapid growth can be attributed to several factors. First, its presses turn out a tremendous volume of attractive, yet free, books and pamphlets. The monthly *Plain Truth* magazine has a circulation of over three million. Second, the growth of this group is stimulated by its three colleges, which have first-class facilities. And third, this cult has reached millions through the effective use of both radio and television.

As this cult has been growing in size, it has been multiplying its influence. Any person or cult which claims the Bible as the highest authority, as does Armstrongism, will make inroads into the true Church of Jesus Christ. Most cults thrive on those they convert out of Christian churches, whether they be liberal or conservative in theology. The immature and carnal are most easily drawn away by the new and devious "winds of doctrine" (Eph. 4:14). However, even believers who have some knowledge of the truth can be affected, since it is not simply the ideas of men that are being propagated, but rather the perversion of doctrine that finds its source in the Wicked One and his followers (I Tim. 4:1).

Armstrongism follows the course of every other cult. It too claims loyalty to God and His Word with the result that it takes both people and money away from the valid work of God. It also brings confusion into the church as it mixes some truth with great portions of error.

This rapid growth and influence of the Worldwide Church of God makes imperative a detailed study of it. With the increasing number of cults, splinter groups and religious organizations, it is impossible for any individual to carefully research all these various groups and still carry on his regular occupation. Since very little study has been devoted to this rapidly growing cult, this book hopefully will help meet a need in the realm of apologetics. To effectively combat error, the error itself must be known and understood.

The Purpose of the Study

The general aim of this study is to analyze and present the system of teaching known as the Worldwide Church of

God, or better known by the name of its founder, Herbert W. Armstrong.

The first and primary purpose of this study will be to give a systematic presentation of the doctrines of Armstrongism. The emphasis will naturally fall upon the major areas of doctrinal deviation, rather than on areas where a position is taken that is close to the orthodox one.

A second aim of this book will be to present the orthodox, biblical position on those major areas of erroneous teaching found in Armstrongism. It is not enough to simply declare its views are heretical, but it is also necessary to present the scriptural position based on solid exegesis and sound hermeneutics.

This study will briefly analyze the hermeneutics of this movement, as a third purpose. It will attempt to discover what guidelines were used in arriving at its interpretations.

Fourth, another goal is to look at the origins of this group in order to see what religious thought and groups influenced the theology of the Worldwide Church of God. All cults claim to have come into existence directly at an impulse from God, either through revelation or illumination. It will, therefore, be one purpose to discover how this cult and its teachings came into existence.

It is not our purpose to attack individual personalities or damage the character of any. Since this movement is so closely tied to its leading personalities, it will be necessary to make reference to them, but the intention is that of analyzing doctrines not personalities.

The Procedure of the Study

The emphasis of this study will be on the doctrinal teachings of the Worldwide Church of God, and this is where most of the time will be devoted. However, before this area is entered into, it is necessary to observe something of the history and background of this movement. Following this background of study, the theological structure of this cult will be studied in detail. After analyzing and refuting the major doctrinal errors, the study will turn to the hermeneutics of Armstrongism in an attempt to discover the methods of interpretation employed in arriving at doctrinal positions.

The Scope of the Study

Considering the volumes of literature being produced by the Worldwide Church of God, a detailed answer to all its teachings and interpretations would be impossible. The number of subjects discussed and the multitude of verses quoted or referred to would require that volumes be written. However, if it is shown that its major areas of belief are wrong, then it is not necessary to deal with all the numerous subpoints in order to show that the entire system is faulty. It will be within the scope of this book to summarize the doctrines within the major divisions of theology, pointing out the most serious departures from the teachings of the Scriptures. It will then be the writer's intention to discuss in detail some of the important doctrinal errors of this group with a scriptural refutation of them.

Some Background Considerations of the Study
Identifying a Cult

Already in this study the Worldwide Church of God has been labeled as a cult. In order to see if this is a valid designation and in order to observe this group in the whole religious picture, it is necessary to give a definition of a cult and observe something of the identifying pattern of cultism.

The dictionary simply states that a cult is a system of religious worship. A cult might well be defined more precisely than this and include the idea that it is a religious system that contradicts or falls short of orthodox Christianity. In his book *Confronting the Cults*, Gordon Lewis has given a workable definition of a cult.

> A cult designates a religious group which claims authorization by Christ and the Bible but neglects or distorts the gospel, the central message of the Savior and the Scriptures.[5]

In analyzing this definition, it is observed that a cult is a religious movement as opposed to one that is purely philosophical or political. Also, it is a religious movement within the broad designation of "Christendom," since it claims the authority of Jesus Christ and the sanction of the Scriptures. The definition further notes that it is a religious group which in some way deviates from historic, orthodox Christianity. This departure takes place when new revelation is added to the body of inscripturated truth; when minor theological points are made central tenets of the faith; and when the fundamental truths of the Christian faith are removed, distorted or redefined. When some or all of these things are true, that religious group within the orb of "Christendom" deserves the classification of a cult. As it will be seen later in the discussion of Armstrong's theology, the Worldwide Church of God fits this definition.

There is also an attitude and approach which is common to cultic groups, which is common as well to Armstrongism. First, the doctrinal structure of a cult is always constructed on the founder of that cult. It is not what the Bible teaches that is really crucial, but rather what he (or she) says it teaches. The founder or leader always receives revelation from God or is blessed with new illumination on many passages of Scripture. The system is built on the founder's teachings which came from this revelation or illumination. Second, cults generally seem to have great respect for the Bible and do not devalue it. Each group claims instead to unlock the truths of the Scriptures to all who will but listen. Most often they will quote volumes of Scripture verses to demonstrate their adherence to the Bible. Third, it is also a characteristic common to cults that they claim to be God's main or sole authority in the world today. Cults feel that traditional churches have long ago left the pure truth of God and by doing so forfeited any right to claim that they are of God. One other trait common to cultic groups is their redefining of the established terminology of biblical Christianity. The theological terms which orthodox Christianity has used for centuries have been given new meanings by these groups. Dr. Walter Martin calls this "theological term-switching." He discusses the semantics of the cults.

> . . . . one must face the fact that the originators and promulgators of cult theology have done exactly the same thing to the semantic structure of Christian theology as did the modern theologians. So Mormon, for example, to utilize the terminology of Biblical Christianity with absolute freedom, having already redesigned these terms in a theological framework of his own making and to his own liking, but almost always at direct variance with the historically accepted meanings of the terms.[6]

> The average non-Christian cult owes its very existence to the fact that it has utilized the terminology of Christianity, has borrowed liberally from the Bible, almost always out of context, and sprinkled its format with evangelical cliches and terms wherever possible or advantageous.[7]

The above description of some common characteristics of a cult is demonstrable in the case of the Worldwide Church of God. Its structure theologically has been built squarely upon the illumination of Herbert W. Armstrong. It too claims allegiance to the Scriptures, yet is guilty of redefining biblical terminology to fit its framework and, as with the others, Armstrongism claims to be God's sole agency on earth today. These characteristics are true of the Worldwide Church of God and clearly place it outside the framework of biblical Christianity and into the camp of the cults.

The Psychology of a Cult

There seems to be a "cult mentality" which can be observed to a greater or lesser degree in all cultic groups. Individuals and groups under the teachings and authority of cults have in common certain psychological traits. In his book, *Kingdom of the Cults,* Dr. Martin discusses four of them. "First, and foremost, the belief systems of the cults are characterized by closed-mindedness."[8] This is true because the individual cultist places himself under the authoritative pronouncements of his group. Logical arguments or facts which contradict the cult's belief system are not allowed to penetrate.

> . . . men are built with an interior demand for outside authority. They want someone to tell them what to do, what to believe, what is right, what is wrong. If they can locate such a definite and detailed authority, it takes away the burden of thinking for themselves.[9]

A second trait is that of antagonism toward the orthodox Christian and his message.

> Secondly, cultic belief systems are characterized by genuine antagonism on a personal level since the cultist almost always identifies his dislike of the Christian message with the messenger who holds such opposing beliefs.[10]

Cults reinforce their position by declaring that the churches of Christendom have incorporated pagan ideas and doctrines into their false systems, which ultimately have their source in Satan. Orthodox ministers are generally viewed as enemies who propagate demonic doctrines which delude their poor, unenlightened followers. These individuals, therefore, are viewed with considerable suspicion.

The claim to supernatural origin (through revelation or illumination) causes authoritative pronouncements by the founder.

> Thirdly, almost without exception cultic belief systems all manifest a type of institutional dogmatism and a pronounced intolerance for any position but their own.[11]

Any deviation from a cult's pronouncements or acceptance of other viewpoints is seen as a departure from the only true faith.

Finally, there is a problem of contradiction within the cult's theological structure. Often positions are held which cannot be justified biblically or logically, and which actually are at variance with one another.

> Within the structure of non-Christian cult systems one can observe the peaceful co-existence of beliefs that are beyond a ques-

tion of a doubt logically contradictory and which in terms of psychological analysis would come under the heading of "compartmentalization."[12]

These four psychological factors are clearly found running throughout the literature of the Worldwide Church of God. Armstrongism, though making the usual claim of uniqueness, nevertheless follows the pattern of all cultism.

The Propaganda Methods of the Worldwide Church of God

Since its inception in 1934, the Worldwide Church of God has experienced tremendous growth, until today its actual membership is said to be around 85,000.[13] According to a recent Armstrong publication this movement expanded by thirty percent each year for the first thirty-five years of its existence, which makes it one of the fastest growing cults in the western world.[14] Many millions throughout the world are being reached with the theology of Armstrongism.[15] Until very recent days, the orthodox church generally gave little attention to this movement, viewing it as relatively insignificant. However, in the past few years there has been an effort made to produce literature exposing the deviations of this group; thus indicating that within orthodoxy many are beginning to feel the effects of the growth and influence of the Worldwide Church of God.

What accounts for this phenomenal growth in less than forty years of existence? Generally speaking the answer is Herbert W. Armstrong himself. He is a promoter and salesman. He was trained as an advertiser and he has used his background and abilities to their fullest in promoting his movement. However, there are some specific factors that account for this growth as well.

"Low Key" Approach to Evangelism

The Worldwide Church of God views itself as the church with the truth, and which offers that truth to anyone who cares to receive it. They do not evangelize from door to door as do the Jehovah's Witnesses. In fact, it repudiates that approach to religion. Over the air waves and in its literature the Worldwide Church of God constantly impresses the audience that it is up to them to make all decisions and nothing is being forced upon them. For example, "personal counsel" is offered to anyone who asks for it, but never will any representative of the church call unless an actual request is made. This approach has appealed to many who are besieged daily with salesmen pressuring them to buy, buy, buy. They do not get the feeling from Armstrongism that they are being sold religion, nor do they feel that someone is taking advantage of them.

The Utilization of Radio and Television

Religious groups, cultic and noncultic, have used these tools of mass media for years, but most have not had the success of the Worldwide Church of God. It is true that most have not had the number or quality of stations as compared with those on which the Worldwide Church broadcasts,[16] but there is more to its success than sheer watts of power.

In a study of the impact of religious radio and television programming on the American public, Haddon W. Robinson has brought together some interesting data.[17] Dr. Robinson states that most religious programs do not really get converts, but rather they tend to simply reinforce the existing beliefs of the listeners. This is true, he says, because the listener generally will not tune in and listen to messages that contradict his personal belief system.

While this would be true of the average religious broadcast, it would not be particularly valid when applied to the broadcasting of the Worldwide Church of God. The Worldwide Church of God differs from the average religious broadcast in a number of ways. First, it has been noted already that the "low key" approach of the Armstrong movement is less inclined to alienate listeners. Religion is not "pushed" by Garner Ted Armstrong, the voice of the Worldwide Church of

God. Second, he discusses many nontheological issues. Most of his time is spent in discussing issues that people are concerned about and want answers to, such as: child-rearing, pollution, crime, managing finances, marriage and divorce. To be sure, doctrinal matters are not completely neglected, but they are never presented in an "offensive" way.

In his study, Dr. Robinson points out that there are some definite advantages to being on radio and television, one being that this raises the credibility and stature of the speaker in a way that literature cannot.

> Lazarfeld and Merton believe that the mass media themselves are invested with a halo of prestige by a large portion of the public, and that by legitimizing the status of individuals and causes, the media can thus bestow prestige on public issues, persons or groups, and social movements.[18]

Robinson further suggests that people are more inclined to believe what they have heard over radio and television than what they have read in print. This is evidently true in the case of Garner Ted Armstrong and the Worldwide Church of God. It is the broadcasts that lend credibility to the movement and attract the inquirers. Charles DeLoach comments on this point.

> With few exceptions, one is first introduced to this sect through *The World Tomorrow* broadcast, which for many years featured the elder Armstrong. The voice of this program now belongs to Garner Ted Armstrong. . . . The voice of the younger Armstrong is an appealing one. It has been described by one veteran of the broadcasting industry as one of the "best voices on radio today." It is the kind of voice that is able to make even a dull subject sound interesting, but, as it happens, that is hardly necessary since most of the material used on the broadcast is fascinating enough in itself.[19]

William C. Martin has written an article in which he discusses, with a great amount of sarcasm, today's radio evangelists. In it he points to many of the ludicrous claims, statements and offers of the numerous religious charlatans, but even he notes that the presentation and content of the programs presented by the Worldwide Church of God is superior to the rest, and is far more successful. He also states,

> In sharp contrast, Garner Ted Armstrong makes it quite clear that all publications offered on his broadcasts are free. There is no gimmick. Those who request literature never receive any hint of an appeal for funds unless they specifically ask how they might contribute to the support of the program. . . . This scrupulous approach has proved quite successful. *The World Tomorrow*, a half-hour program, is heard daily on more than four hundred stations throughout the world, and a television version is carried by sixty stations.[20]

Mr. Martin's comment has brought up the next point in the discussion of Armstrongism's success factors.

The Giving of Quality Literature

No request is ever made of a nonmember to give money to the Worldwide Church of God. Literature is available for the asking. The literature itself is printed on high quality paper, with an eye-pleasing format, and often with full color pictures. The receiving of this literature never brings any obligation on the part of the recipient. These pamphlets find their way into millions of homes.

> More than a million have received the booklet concerning crime, the *causes* of it, and how, without resorting to joining pressure groups or becoming activists, to protect themselves, their children and their property from criminals.[21]

This pamphlet on crime is but one of dozens printed and sent in volume to the asking public. Although no "follow up" is ever made, this invitation of free literature has been the bait to draw many into the movement, as a former Armstrongite testifies.

> No doubt many people wonder how a person comes to be an Armstrongite. Many readers of Mr. Armstrong's literature do not fully grasp the fact that every article or book distributed by him is designed as a lure with which to lead its readers into his church.[22]

The literature offered by this group discusses a wide variety of subjects from marijuana to pyramidology. A great number of theological subjects are available to any inquirer. These subjects appear in *The Plain Truth* and *Tomorrow's World* magazines (now under one cover, as *The Plain Truth*).[23] Also booklets and reprints of important articles are available.

The real work of indoctrination begins when a person sends away for the free Bible correspondence course. It is here that the unwary reader is led step by programmed step through the doctrines of Armstrognism. In the study courses, questions are asked in connection with verses that are listed in the study. It is interesting to observe that usually the answer is given or implied in the question. If the reader doesn't pick it up there, a "comment" is added which helps bring home the "truth" with utmost clarity. It is advertised as an opportunity for an individual to study the Bible for himself, but it is in reality a stiff indoctrination program. 80,000 are enrolled in this correspondence course, many of whom are not members of the Worldwide Church of God.[24]

The Training of Members

The Worldwide Church of God knows the value of training its own, and has therefore established three colleges. It is convinced that the Great Commission is an educational message of the way of life to be lived in the Kingdom of God.[25] There is the understanding that people trained in the ways of Armstrongism are a must if the work is going to expand.

Members are indoctrinated by studying and restudying the booklets and the correspondence lessons. They must attend Saturday services each week and attend regular study meetings as often as possible. They are to attend the special Holy Day meetings, plus be involved in other activities of the church.[26]

Exploiting Today's Unrest

In this world today there is still that "God-shaped vacuum" in men that needs to be filled, but most churches in twentieth century America are trying to fill it with coffee and donuts. Armstrongism has seized upon the religious bankruptcy that characterizes many "Christian" churches today and has rightly pointed out that people are getting nothing satisfying from these places. The people themselves realize this and many are impressed with Armstrongism's apparent loyalty to and preaching of the Bible.

> In an age of religious apostasy, in which millions of Bible-believing Christians have lost confidence in their denominational leaders and institutions, Herbert W. Armstrong has declared himself and his church to be unequivocally committed to the inspiration and inerrancy of Scripture. He has projected an image of unwavering orthodoxy by affirming the deity, virgin birth, vicarious death, glorification, and pre-millennial return of Jesus Christ.[27]

After being constantly exposed to the ambiguous, soul-withering philosophies of many clergymen, people find Armstrong's "thus saith" a welcome change. It is certainly not a true "thus saith the Lord," but many are attracted by the authoritative stance taken by this movement.

Armstrongism has stood firm for high moral values and has attacked the creeping moral corruption of western society.

> In a day of moral decay and spiritual poverty, Armstrong has scathingly condemned the new morality, biblical illiteracy, the drug menace, divorce, the hippie culture, the militant protest movements, women's lib, pollution, inflation and other aspects of society today that many feel are warning signs of the demise of civilization.
>
> In a time of cynical repudiation of moral values, Armstrong has vigorously affirmed the old-fashioned Christian and American virtues of honor, reverence, patriotism, thrift, integrity, chastity and temperance. Thus he has gained the sympathy and support of vast numbers of the so-called silent majority.[28]

It is the feeling of others, however, that fear is one of the main tools of Armstrongism in its attempt to win converts: fear of the future both personally and globally. People are said to be frightened into the kingdom by the vivid pictures of future horrors that are painted by the Armstrong cult. This is the evaluation of Richard Marson, an ex-Armstrongite.

However, other literature is greatly concerned with future prophecy in the light of present world news. Some of these news and
prophetic messages contain elements of a fear psychology.[29]

Many people realize that the tools of a good salesman, among
others, are attempts to arouse desire for the product on the part
of the buyer, and worrying him into fearing adverse results from
failure to buy. Mr. Armstrong is very well acquainted with the
tools of a good salesman.[30]

Tithing of the Membership

Members are required to give at least one-tenth of their
earnings and often a double or triple tithe is called for. The
impression is given in the magazines that the "co-workers"
freely give to support the work. While it is undoubtedly true
that many thousands do, it is also evident that the member
who fails to give his tithe finds himself in serious trouble with
the church. Approximately thirty-five million dollars annual-
ly comes into the church's treasury, of which about seventy
percent comes from the tithing members.[31]

Although nonmembers are never asked to give, it is also
true that many thousands do send in gifts anyway. Perhaps
feeling gratitude that there is some organization that wants to
help them and not get their money, they end up sending in
more money than if they were charged for the booklets.

Conclusion

These six factors have contributed to the great growth of
this movement. The effective use of the mass media and the
offer of free literature has drawn many people into Armstrongism, and the training received afterwards has kept most
of them there. It should always be remembered, however,
that the personalities of Herbert and Garner Ted Armstrong
are the guiding forces behind this entire movement. Both
seem to possess that indefinable quality called "charisma,"
and there would be no powerful Worldwide Church of God
today without them. Certainly too, the Bible informs us that
behind human personalities who propagate heresy, there is

the personality of the Wicked One whose sole purpose now is to thwart the will of God. This Satan does by duplicating closely the work of God in this world. He has constructed a marvelous counterfeit in the Worldwide Church of God.

A Brief History of the Worldwide Church of God

No movement, religious or otherwise, comes into existence out of a vacuum, free from outside influences. The personalities involved carry their personal experiences and background along with them into the movement. Past systems of belief and thought are seen reflected in the present system to some degree, and what is claimed as new is often nothing more than a new revision of the old. In viewing the history and background of the Worldwide Church of God, it will be seen that both the personality of its founder and the religious concepts of others are indeed reflected in this movement.

The Personalities Behind the Worldwide Church of God

The Role of Herbert W. Armstrong

There is no doubt whatever that there would be no Worldwide Church of God if it were not for Herbert Armstrong. He is the founder, "prophet," and dominant influence behind this movement. He has brought it from its obscure beginning to a position of prominence and power. Whether the same growth and outward unity of this movement will continue past his death is an uncertainty.

Herbert Armstrong was born in Des Moines, Iowa on July 31, 1892. His childhood days were spent in a number of towns in Iowa according to his autobiography.[1] In his late teenage years, Mr. Armstrong decided that he was best suited for the field of advertising. He comments:

> I had no conception, then, that the advertising profession was not, after all, to be my final profession—or that this experience was merely the preliminary training needed for the ultimate bigger job in God's ministry.[2]

Although he had very little formal education, his personal drive enabled him to do well in advertising and to develop an ability in this field. He endured several business failures as well as enjoyed successes and Armstrong sees these years in the advertising profession as extremely important.

> All this advertising instruction was the most valuable possible training for the real mission in life to-which I was later to be called—God's world-wide ministry. It was a training such as one could never receive in any university or theological seminary. It was the most practical training *for preaching,* as well as for *writing* Gospel messages.[3]

There is no doubt that what he learned in those years has been put into practice today in the promoting of his doctrines. His magazines, *The Plain Truth* and *Tomorrow's World* (now united under one cover), reflect his earlier training in their style and format. Also, the various pamphlets and the correspondence course give evidence of his background. They appeal to the reader's eye, creating a desire in him to continue on page after page. Leading questions, pictures, and a variety of type faces are employed in order to capture reader interest.

> But in writing advertising, Mr. Boreman taught me always to tell a *story*—to make it *interesting*—and to tell it in *story form.* That is, first, put a question in the minds of readers they really want answered—or make a statement that is so unusual it either raises a question in the readers' minds, or challenges them to demand an explanation and want to read on to get it. It must arouse instant *interest.* It must create *suspense!*[4]

Anyone familiar with his publications sees these elements plainly. The same principles are applied by Armstrong in his radio and television broadcasts.

> It applies to sermons or religious broadcasts, the same as to commercial advertising! I have found that far more people will listen to a solid half-hour all-speech broadcast applying these principles—

a full half-hour SERMON over the air—then will listen to a 5-to-15 minute DRY talk that does not arouse their interest, surrounded and embellished by a lot of music.

THAT EARLY TRAINING, IN VOCABULARY, IN A RAP-ID, LUCID, FAST-MOVING, DYNAMIC WRITING STYLE, WAS THE VERY TRAINING NEEDED FOR THE WORK IN GOD'S MINISTRY! That's why, though I knew nothing of it then, God was steering my formative years into a training I never could have obtained had I gone through the customary universities and theological seminaries.[5]

Mr. Armstrong viewed himself during those years as a cocky, conceited young man.[6] He believed that God had to deal him many heavy blows financially in order to humble him and prepare him for the ministry.

Mr. Armstrong tells his readers that as a child he regularly attended Sunday School at the First Friends Church in Des Moines. In this connection he mentions his ancestry, reflecting his British-Israelite thinking.

Both my father and mother were of solid Quaker stock. My ancestors came to America with William Penn, a hundred years before the United States became a nation. Indeed I have the genealogy of my ancestors back to Edward I of England, and through the British Royal genealogy, back to King Herremon of Ireland who married the Queen Tea Tephi, daughter of Zedekiah, King of Judah.[7]

His interest in religion decreased during his teenage years, about the time he entered the advertising field. After his marriage, he and his wife periodically attended church, but religion was meaningless to him. However, it was in 1926 that things changed radically as far as religious conviction was concerned. After moving to Salem, Oregon, Mrs. Armstrong became acquainted with an elderly neighbor lady who led her to a belief in the need to keep the seventh-day Sabbath. This ignited religious controversy in the Armstrong household, which led to Herbert Armstrong's personal study of the Bible. After this study, he concluded that the Sabbath was indeed the seventh day and it was to be observed. Other conclusions were reached which pointed Armstrong in the direction that would eventually lead to the founding of the Worldwide Church of God.

> It was humiliating to have to admit my wife had been right, and I had been wrong. It was disillusioning to learn, on studying the Bible for the first time that what I had been taught in Sunday School was, in so many basic instances, the very opposite of what the Bible plainly states. It was shocking to learn that "all these churches *were* wrong" after all![8]

After concluding that the Bible was not the source of many teachings of the churches, Mr. Armstrong then decided that these teachings originated in the erroneous philosophies of men.

> . . . I found that the popular church teachings and practices were *not* based on the Bible. They had originated, as research in history had revealed, in paganism. Numerous Bible prophecies foretold it. The amazing, unbelievable TRUTH was, the SOURCE of these popular beliefs and practices of professing Christianity was, quite largely, paganism and human reasoning and custom, NOT *the Bible!*[9]

Mr. Armstrong points to January, 1934 as the beginning of the Worldwide Church of God (known then as the Radio Church of God). It was right about this time that he declares that the "Sardis" era of the church was over and the "Philadelphia" era began, "Philadelphia" being a reference to his movement.[10] He began both the radio broadcast and the publishing of *The Plain Truth* at this time.

The work of Herbert Armstrong continued to grow in Oregon until the decision was made to move to California.

> By 1946 we were outgrowing facilities available in Eugene, Oregon. It was becoming imperative that the Work be moved accessible to Hollywood—radio headquarters for the nation. At the same time, we began to realize that future expansion of the Work demanded a college for the training of expanding personnel. There were many reasons why we selected Pasadena as our future site.[11]

The Pasadena campus of Ambassador College continued to grow as more land and buildings were added. Today it is the center of the printing and broadcasting work of the Worldwide Church of God. Later two more colleges were founded to train young people in the doctrines of the Worldwide Church of God.

> From the founding of the college in Pasadena, branch colleges abroad were envisioned. . . . Finally, in 1959, a suitable property was purchased for the campus in Britain, some five miles from the outskirts of Greater London, . . . the English campus, near St. Albans, was opened to students in 1960. The Texas campus opened in September, 1964.[12]

The Worldwide Church of God is growing rapidly. The June, 1974 issue of the *Plain Truth* was sent to over two and a half million readers. It is estimated that fifty million listeners tune in weekly to the World Tomorrow broadcast.[13] The program is being carried on some three hundred radio stations and over sixty television stations.[14] Thousands are being indoctrinated through the Bible correspondence course, and there are some two hundred and fifty local congregations where Armstrongism is being preached.[15] The Worldwide Church of God is growing and the dynamic personality of Herbert W. Armstrong has been the guiding force behind it.

The Role of Garner Ted Armstrong

Garner Ted Armstrong was born in Oregon on February 9, 1930. He was Herbert Armstrong's fourth child, and second son.[16] He explains that he did not simply adopt his father's religion, but rather was ashamed of it and wanted little to do with it, looking instead to the entertainment world for his future.

> I continually ran from *hearing* the truth. My mind was closed. I had *never read,* believe it or not, ONE of the booklets my father had written. Oh, I suppose I had skimmed lightly through one or two of the many . . . I never read the PLAIN TRUTH magazine. That was just something "DAD was doing."[17]
> I was on the waiting list for page boy at CBS, in Hollywood and had tried out in two auditions for TV talent shows. My goal was television, or the movies, or failing these, nightclub entertainment.[18]

He goes on to explain that through personal Bible study and inner struggle he finally came to the conclusion that what his father was teaching was what the Bible really taught. After repentance and baptism, he was eventually led into the work of the Worldwide Church of God.

> And that is how it REALLY happened. Looking back—I know I was being PUT into Christ's work. I didn't CHOOSE it. I didn't just "go along" with my father's "organization." I was CALLED into it—was PUT into it.[19]

It seems as though this was written as an apologetic to avoid the charge of nepotism, but whatever is the case, Garner Ted Armstrong has become the vice-chancellor of Ambassador College in Pasadena, the vice-president of the entire movement and the national broadcaster of the Worldwide Church of God.

Early in the year 1972 Garner Ted Armstrong was snared by problems which caused him to be stripped of his titles and responsibilities.[20] The problems seemed to be resolved and he returned to the air for the Worldwide Church of God in June of the same year. However, the problems have since revived, causing schism in the movement (see Appendix).

The Religious Thinking Which Influenced the Worldwide Church of God
The Religious History of Its Founder

Although something of the life of Herbert Armstrong has been given, several other points need to be made. His call to "The Work" is of interest. He was ordained by the Oregon Conference of the Church of God, but received an angelic call through his wife earlier in life. He says,

> One night my wife had a dream so vivid and impressive it overwhelmed and shook her tremendously. It was so realistic it seemed more like a vision. . . . "Then it seemed He had changed into an angel. I was terribly disappointed at first, but then he told me Christ was really coming in a very short time."
>
> I have only come to believe that this dream was a bona fide call from God in the light of subsequent events.[21]
>
> My wife saw an angel *revealing* that God was calling me and her to the mission of warning this world. . . .

No doubt the inclusion of this by Mr. Armstrong is an attempt to add authenticity to his movement. However, the evangelical Christian immediately becmes suspicious of such claims.

Concerning his past associations with other religious bodies, Herbert Armstrong categorically denies any past affiliation with Seventh-day Adventism or the Jehovah's Witnesses.

> I have never been a member of the "Jehovah's Witnesses," nor of the Seventh-day Adventists. I have never in any manner, shape, or form had any remote connection with them, or associated with either sect or denomination. I have never had fellowship with them.[22]

His early associations were with a small Sabbath observing group. He identified himself with the Church of God (Stanberry, Missouri) and was baptized and ordained by this group. However, this Church of God group was in reality an offshoot of Adventism.

> This small group was actually an early offshoot of the Seventh-day Adventist Church. In 1866 Elders B. F. Snook and W. H. Brinkerhoff apostacized from the Iowa Conference of the Seventh-day Adventists and led off a number of people to form this independent group, referred to among Seventh-day Adventists as "the Marion Party" (from Marion, Iowa, their original headquarters). In 1889 they moved to Stanberry, Missouri, where they operated a small publishing house and called their paper *The Bible Advocate*. They used the name "Church of God (Adventist)" for a time, and later became known as "The Church of God (Seventh Day)."[23]

Technically, then, Herbert Armstrong can claim that he had no association with Seventh-day Adventism, but in reality he was exposed to Adventist teachings for several years — formative years, at that.

Because of his writings, Mr. Armstrong began having conflict with the Stanberry group. The primary issues seem to have been over Armstrong's ideas on the Old Testament feast days and British-Israelism.

> Several years ago this man was a minister of our faith. However,

> he jumped the track on British-Israelism, and a few other con-
> nected subjects . . .[24]
>
> Mr. Armstrong became convinced, through his own personal
> Bible study, that the Feast Days are still to be kept by Christians
> today. He wanted to preach this doctrine, and this resulted in his
> ministerial license being revoked by the Oregon Conference
> Board.[25]

Herbert Armstrong, along with some others, left the Stanberry group in 1933 and formed yet another group. He affiliated with this new group for several years.

> It was in the year 1933 when Elder Armstrong separated from
> Stanberry and went along with about 100 or more ministers
> organizing the church at Salem (West Virginia) on the Bible foun-
> dation of church organization, with the twelve, the seventy, and
> the seven. He became one of the seventy, at that time, chosen so
> by lot. He remained in this place for a few years . . . he broke
> with the Salem organization over the keeping of the yearly sab-
> baths set forth in Leviticus, 23rd chapter.[26]

Finally, after this, Herbert Armstrong went completely
independent and established his own church which is known
today as the Worldwide Church of God.

The Influence of Other Religious Groups and Thoughts
The Claims of Herbert Armstrong

The claims and statements of Herbert Armstrong and the
Worldwide Church of God are both confusing and at times
contradictory. It has been noted in Chapter 1 that it is a
common characteristic of cultism to claim to have the keys
that unlock biblical truth, and because of this claim they
view themselves as God's main or sole authority on the earth.
The "truth" they possess has had its source in their founder,
who supposedly got it directly from God either through revelation or illumination. In the case of Herbert Armstrong, he
claims a form of illumination which intrudes into the realm
of revelation. Some quotations by him and about him show
this emphasis.

> The Gospel which is preached by me is NOT AFTER MAN, for I
> neither received it of man, neither was I taught it but BY THE

REVELATION OF JESUS CHRIST. He revealed it to me in HIS WRITTEN WORD! Then when it pleased God, who called me by His GRACE, to reveal His Son in me, that I might preach Him to the world.[27]

Jesus chose Paul, who was highly educated, for spreading the gospel to the Gentiles. He later raised up Peter Waldo, a successful businessman, to keep His truth alive during the Middle Ages. In these last days WHEN THE GOSPEL MUST GO AROUND THE WORLD, Jesus chose a man amply trained in the advertising and business fields to shoulder the mission—HERBERT W. ARMSTRONG.[28]

By God's direction and authority, I have laid the TRUTH before you! To neglect it will be tragic beyond imagination.[29]

But Christ also foretold that, *just before* the END of *this* world—*this* age— . . . His very *same* Gospel of God's KINGDOM "shall be preached" (Matt. 24:14) and also *published* (Mark 13: 10) . . . And at last, in the light of fast-developing, world-encircling events it became apparent that what was actually happening, back in 1934, was precisely this: Jesus Christ (Rev. 3:8) was opening the gigantic mass-media DOOR of radio and the printing press for the proclaiming of His same original GOSPEL to all the world![30]

Also their leader had confessed . . . that new biblical TRUTH had been revealed to me, yet he and the Church rejected this truth and later persecuted me because I did accept and proclaim it.[31]

And, knowing that such an unbelievable catastrophe is soon to strike, I HAVE TO WARN YOU! You can read what God says to *me* in Ezekiel 33:1-6.[32]

These quotations give striking evidence of the importance placed on the man himself as well as on his revelatory illumination. However, Mr. Armstrong emphatically states that he is not a prophet, like those of old who received new revelation from God.

Thousands know that I, personally, have been called and chosen for a very definite commission in God's service. But I definitely have NOT been called to be a PROPHET. . . . Emphatically I am NOT a prophet, in the sense of one to whom God speaks specially and directly, revealing personally a future event to happen or new truth, or new and special instruction direct from God—separate from, and apart from what is contained in the Bible.[33]

However, in spite of his denials, the fact still remains that he does claim that new truth, embedded in the Bible, has been revealed in him. He makes it clear that he received none of his doctrine from men. He does insist that all revelation has been written down in the Scriptures, but all this is essentially negated by his claims of illumination. Though he rejects the title of prophet, he clearly views himself as a unique and key individual in God's program. This is brought out most forcibly in his autobiography where he compares and parallels his life and ministry with the life and work of the Lord.[34]

Two main facts come out of a study of the claims of Herbert Armstrong. First, his illumination is, in reality, a form of revelation. Second, he denies any indebtedness to the religious concepts, ideas or interpretations of other men. This denial will now be analyzed in more detail by observing some teachings of Armstrong and comparing them with those of other groups.

A Comparison of Teachings

It is the conviction of all outside of the Worldwide Church of God, who have studied its system, that it is eclectic. Although refusing to admit this, the Worldwide Church of God has evidently borrowed, incorporated and revised doctrines from others and brought them into its system. It cannot legitimately say that it holds the key to the truth of the Scriptures, while at the same time holding to the identical teachings of other groups. The credibility of such assertions is suspect. This is especially true when the other systems were on the religious scene years before the founding of the Worldwide Church of God. On this point Chambers makes a valid observation.

> . . . the pivotal issue is not the question of the accuracy of his system of biblical interpretation, but the question of its absolute uniqueness. There is no *logical* necessity of proving that the key does not fit the lock in order to brand Armstrong a deceiver. There is only the necessity of proving that the key has not been lost since the time of the apostles.[35]

This statement was made in the context of a discussion on Armstrong's British-Israelite theory which is not original with him. It is our concern, however, to view his entire system.

It is not the purpose of this section to give a detailed study of theology, but rather to show that the supposedly unique doctrines of the Worldwide Church of God bear an amazing resemblance to the doctrines of other groups. It is this writer's contention that the closeness of teaching clearly indicates Armstrong's familiarity with and incorporation of the doctrines of other men. He *has* been influenced by them.

The Influence of Seventh-day Adventism

It was noted previously that Herbert Armstrong was affiliated for several years with the Church of God (Seventh-day), which is an offshoot of Seventh-day Adventism. The influence of Adventism is readily apparent by comparing quotations from Armstrong's writings and those of Adventist writers, and Mr. Armstrong himself admits studying much of their literature.[36]

In comparing these teachings, a quote will be given from the literature of the Worldwide Church of God, followed by a quotation from a Seventh-day Adventist source. The subject of the quotation will precede them.

Sabbath keeping is a command and a sign today.

> But throughout the Bible, God commands true Christians to worship Him by observing the day *He* made holy—the seventh-day Sabbath! Observance of the true Sabbath is the SIGN between God and His true people. . . .[37]
>
> Nowhere in all Scripture is there even a hint of Sabbath change. God's moral law is the foundation of the new covenant as it was of the old. This new covenant calls for faithful obedience just as did the old. . . . Christian Sabbath keepers rest in the assurance that because they love to obey God's changeless law, written in their hearts under new-covenant terms, they carry in their lives the *sign* of God's acceptance.[38]

Sabbath keeping is necessary for salvation.

> Thus did God reveal *which day* is HIS SABBATH, and also that it DOES MAKE LIFE-AND-DEATH DIFFERENCE—for to break God's Holy Sabbath is SIN, and the penalty is eternal DEATH.[39]
>
> One of the conditions of salvation and having our names retained in the book of life, is to keep the Sabbath.[40]

Sunday observance is the "mark of the beast."

> Sunday observance—this is the Mark of the Beast . . . If you are branded with this Mark, rejecting the sign of God (the Sabbath), in your forehead and your hand, you shall be tormented by God's plagues without mercy. Yes, you![41]
>
> Sunday-keeping is an institution of the first beast, and *all* who submit to obey this institution emphatically worship the first beast and receive his mark, "the mark of the beast". . . .[42]

It should be noted at this point that modern Seventh-day Adventists have softened their stand on this issue, viewing the "mark" for Sunday observance as a future thing only.[43] However, in the days when Herbert Armstrong was affiliated with them, the above position was the one held.

Keeping the Ten Commandments is necessary for salvation.

> For if you make any claim to being a Christian . . . you must walk according to the *commandments* of Almighty God if you would enter into eternal life (Matt. 19:17).[46]
>
> A Christian who through faith in Jesus Christ has faithfully kept the law's requirements will be acquitted; there is no condemnation, for the law finds no fault in him. If . . . it is found that one has broken even a single percent . . . he will be dealt with just as if he had broken all ten.[47]

A distinction is made between moral and ceremonial law.

> Faith, the atonement, the gift of the Holy Spirit, DID take the place of, and therefore, abolish the old Mosaic law. That was a law of physical ordinances, ceremonies, and sacrifices. . . . But the Ten Commandments are an entirely different, separate, distinct Law. The Commandments are spiritual principles which define sin. Moses' laws were sacrificial and ceremonial.[48]
>
> The Ten Commandments, or the Decalogue, constitute God's eternal law. Not only is this law eternal, but it is immutable. . . . But while this is true of the eternal law of God as expressed in the the Decalogue, it would not be true of the ceremonial law that God gave to Israel . . . all that was typical of the sacrifice and ministry of Christ our Lord—met its end on Calvary's cross.[49]

Man does not possess a soul.

> Man *became* a living SOUL; that is what man IS—a *soul*. Notice there is no mention that man has a soul, but that man *is* a soul.[50]
>
> This basic idea of "soul" being the individual rather than a constituent *part* of the individual seems to underlie the various occurrences of *nephesh*. It is therefore more accurate to say that a certain person *is* a soul than to say he *has* a soul.[51]

Man is mortal and temporal only.

The life of *man* and the life of *animals* is the same! MORTAL life! . . . The soul of man, therefore, is kept alive by the coursing of blood through his veins.[52]

. . . the Scriptures teach that the soul of man represents the whole man, and not a particular part independent of the other component parts of man's nature; and further, that the soul cannot exist apart from the body, for man is a unit.[53]

Immortality for man is conditional.

In each case, immortality is something that is *brought to light*, that must be *obtained*, that God ONLY has, and in no case is something man already possesses! . . . The *only* way to live for all eternity is to REPENT. . . .[54]

Seventh-day Adventists do not believe that the whole man or any part of him is inherently immortal. We believe the Bible picture of man is of a creature subject to death, with the possibility of eternal life because Christ has paid the penalty for sin and offers *His life* to the repentant sinner.[55]

Death brings cessation of being and "sleep" to man.

Peter preached the RESURRECTION! He said NOTHING about the completely PAGAN doctrine of any . . . going to "hell" or "heaven" when one dies! . . . There is the real TRUTH about death. . . . Death is DEATH—without consciousness.[56]

That man "sleeps" between death and the resurrection is the express testimony of Scripture.[57]

Christ could have sinned as a man.

Jesus constantly had to CRY OUT to God *day and night* to keep Himself from falling! . . . the tremendous *battle*, the lifelong *struggle* Christ had with *Himself*, in overcoming His own human nature—the natural pulls of the flesh. . . .[58]

Many claim that it was impossible for Christ to be overcome by temptation. Then He could not have been placed in Adam's position; . . . But our Saviour took humanity, with all its liabilities. He took the nature of man, with the possibility of yielding to temptation.[59]

The new birth is connected with the resurrection, and is a process.

The experience of conversion, in this life, is a *begettal*—a "conception"—an "impregnation"—but NOT YET A BIRTH. . . . That tremendous, glorious event of being BORN of God is to take place AT THE RESURRECTION OF THE JUST—at the time of

> Christ's second coming to earth! . . . All true Christians who have
> died before Christ's coming shall rise first—in a resurrection—and
> then all Christians *still alive,* in mortal flesh, shall be instanta-
> neously—in the twinkling of an eye . . . at last BORN OF GOD![60]

> . . . the new birth comprises the entire change necessary to fit
> us for the kingdom of God, and consists of two parts: First, a
> moral change wrought by conversion and a Christian life (John
> 3:5); second, a physical change at the second coming of Christ,
> whereby, if dead, we are raised incorruptible, and if living, are
> changed to immortality in a moment, in the twinkling of an eye.
> Luke 20:36; I Corinthians 15:51, 52.[61]

The Worldwide Church of God has carried this idea of new
birth far beyond the Seventh-day Adventists, teaching that
men become divine when they are born again at the resurrection, but, nevertheless, the seed thought of the new birth
being a process which is completed at the resurrection is to
be found in Adventism.

Other parallels between Armstrongism and Adventism
could be made in their teachings of the human nature of
Christ, the atonement of Christ, the definition of sin, individual eschatology, abstinence from certain foods and in the
interpretation of specific Scripture passages. However, the
above should give a clear indication of the influence of
Seventh-day Adventism on Herbert W. Armstrong's theology.

The Influence of the Jehovah's Witnesses

Though Herbert Armstrong never affiliated with the
Jehovah's Witnesses, he did become familiar with their literature. He claims, however, that he had come to the truth
before finding out that they agreed on points with him. The
similarity of teaching and argumentation between the two
challenges the credibility of this assertion, since Charles Taze
Russell lived and wrote long before the theology of the
Worldwide Church of God was formulated.

Some comparisons will be made, following the same
pattern as above. First a quotation from the Worldwide
Church of God followed by a statement from the Jehovah's
Witnesses.

The "trinity" is a pagan concept.

But the theologians and "Higher Critics" have blindly accepted the heretical and false doctrine introduced by PAGAN false prophets who crept in, that the HOLY SPIRIT is a THIRD PERSON—the heresy of the "TRINITY."[62]

The origin of the trinity doctrine is traced back to the ancient Babylonians and Egyptians and other ancient mythologists. . . . It thus came to be declared the doctrine of the religious organization of Christendom, and the clergy have ever held to this complicated doctrine.[63]

The Holy Spirit is a force, not a person.

God's Spirit, which is not a person, but the *power of God,* the "down payment" of begettal. . . .[64]

So the holy spirit is the invisible active force of Almighty God which moves his servants to do his will.[65]

Jesus Christ rose in a spiritual, not a material body.

Nowhere does the Scripture say He was alive and active, or that God had Him get back into the human BODY that had died. . . . And the resurrected body was no longer human . . . it was the Christ resurrected IMMORTAL, once *again* CHANGED![66]

On the third day of his being dead in the grave his immortal Father Jehovah God raised him from the dead, not as a human Son, but as a mighty immortal spirit Son. . . .[67]

The Worldwide Church of God teaches that Christians will be raised spirit beings because they will be like Christ. Concerning Jesus, it is said, "After His resurrection, Jesus was invisible."[68]

The wicked will be annihilated.

This death is for ALL ETERNITY—ETERNAL PUNISHMENT— but it is *not* eternal punishing![69]

Since God destroys soul and body in Gehenna, this is conclusive proof that Gehenna . . . is a picture or symbol of complete annihilation, and not of eternal torment. . . . So the everlasting punishment of the "goats" is their everlastingly being cut off from all life.[70]

An opportunity for salvation after death.

And finally a resurrection of all who have ever lived—those who have *never* had *any chance,* who have *never been called* by the Father—every human being who has ever lived to be brought back to life and given that *one and only* opportunity God ever gives everyone to become His Son![71]

. . . the "resurrection of judgment" is for those persons whose hearts may have been wanting to do right, but who died without ever having an opportunity to hear. . . . These people will be brought back into the paradise earth. They will be taught the truth. They will be shown what is right.[72]

Other teachings of the two groups are similar, including some in the area of eschatology and the work of Christ.

The Influence of Mormonism

No mention is made by Mr. Armstrong of his familiarity with the Mormon literature. However, some teachings are strikingly similar.

Deity is the ultimate goal for men.

The PURPOSE of life is that in us God is really re-creating His own kind—reproducing Himself after His own kind—for we are, upon real conversion, actually begotten as sons (yet unborn) of God; . . . we grow spiritually more and more like God, until, at the time of the resurrection we shall be instantaneously changed from mortal into immortal—we shall then be born of God—WE SHALL THEN BE GOD![73]

We believe in a God who is Himself progressive, whose majesty is intelligence; . . . a Being who has attained His exalted state by a path which now His children are permitted to follow, whose glory it is their heritage to share. In spite of the opposition of the sects, in the face of direct charges of blasphemy, the Church proclaims the eternal truth: *"As man is, God once was; as God is, man may be."*[74]

The Fall was a good thing and was planned by God.

God knew that Adam would react to a given situation in the same general manner as every other human would react to that same situation. As Adam "went" so all mankind would "go." God *designed* human nature to be vain, jealous, lustful, greedy, and antagonistic to God. . . . So Adam sinned and hid himself from God—precisely conforming to God's specifications.[75]

It was the purpose of God to place within the reach of the spirits begotten by Him in the heavens the means of individual efforts, and the opportunity of winning not merely redemption from death but also salvation and even exhaltation, with the powers of eternal progression and increase. Hence it was necessary that the spiritual offspring of God should leave the scenes of their primeval childhood and enter the school of mortal experience, meeting, contending with, and overcoming evil. . . . Eve was fulfilling the foreseen purposes of God by the part she took in the great drama of the fall . . . our first parents are entitled to our deepest gratitude for their legacy to posterity—the means of winning title to glory, exhaltation and eternal lives.[76]

The true church has been lost since the days of the apostles.

. . . A.D. 69, the Apostles and the Church fled to Pella from Jerusalem according to Jesus' warning (Matt. 24:15, 16). That was the END of the organized proclaiming of Christ's Gospel by His Church to the world! . . . For 18½ centuries all worldwide organized proclaiming of *Christ's Gospel* was stamped out. . . .[77]

From the facts already stated it is evident that the Church was literally driven from the earth. . . . But the Lord in His mercy provided the reestablishment of His Church in the last days, and for the last time; . . . This restoration was effected by the Lord through the Prophet Joseph Smith. . . .[78]

The name "Elohim" shows a plurality of Gods.

And as I have explained previously, God is not a single person, but the Hebrew word for God, *Elohim,* portrays God as a FAMILY of persons . . . a *single* family or *kingdom,* but composed of MORE than one person.[79]

In the very beginning the Bible shows there is a plurality of God beyond the power of refutation. It is a great subject I am dwelling on. The word *Elohim* ought to be in the plural all the way through—Gods. The heads of the Gods appointed one God for us; and when you take (that) view of the subject, it sets one free to see all the beauty, holiness and perfection of the Gods.[80]

Though the emphasis is somewhat different, both groups use this word as the foundation for their teaching that righteous men will eventually join the Godhead.

These two groups have similar teachings in other areas also such as that of baptismal regeneration.

The Influence of British-Israelism.

British-Israelism differs from the above mentioned groups, because it in and of itself is not a separate cult. Rather, this theory can be incorporated into systems without greatly affecting basic biblical truths such as the Trinity, the substitutionary work of Christ or the inspiration of the Scriptures. It can also be brought into a system which distorts many of the fundamentals of the Scriptures.

The theory of British-Israelism (or Anglo-Israelism) flourished in the 1800's, decades before the "conversion" of Herbert W. Armstrong and the beginning of his movement. The alleged new truth of the Worldwide Church of God parallels in detail the old British-Israelite theory. A few selected quotations will be sufficient to demonstrate this point.

The word "Jew" always means one from Judah.

> Remember that the term "Jew" is merely a nickname for "Judah." Hence, it applies to the one nation, or House of Judah ONLY.[81]

> Hence it is that the names Jew or Jews are applied *only* to the people who compose the kingdom of Judah.[82]

Jews and Israelites are to be distinguished.

> Jews are Israelites, just as Californians are Americans. But MOST Israelites are *not* Jews, just as most Americans are *not* Californians. The Jews are the House of Judah *only*, a PART of the Israelites.[83]

> Understand us: we do not say that the Jews are not Israelites. . . . But the great bulk of Israelites are not the Jews, just as the great bulk of Americans are not Californians, and yet all Californians are Americans.[84]

The "birthright concept" has been a hidden truth for centuries.

> Of course it is well understood that the Sceptre went to Judah, and was handed down through the Jews. . . . But the promises which the Bible terms "the BIRTHRIGHT" have not been understood at all. Few have understood the nature of the Birthright promises.[85]

> That the Sceptre blessing, privileges, and promises pertain to Judah . . . is well known. . . . But that which is called the Birthright has not, in the past, been understood at all, and as yet is understood but by the few.[86]

Jeremiah's call was to Israel in captivity in the British Isles as well as to Judah in the land.

> Notice, Jeremiah was set over NATIONS—more than one kingdom—He was set a prophet over Judah—but not Judah *alone*. Over NATIONS—over KINGDOMS! . . . Jeremiah was set over

not just the *one* nation, JUDAH—but over NATIONS. Over the KINGDOMS—the Kingdom of ISRAEL as well as Judah![87]

Called as the prophet of God . . . and set by the Divine One "over the nations and over the kingdoms." What! Surely he was not set over *all* the nations. . . . He now calls Jeremiah a Prophet unto the nations . . . Israel and Judah.[88]

Jeremiah had a double commission given by God.

It is well known that Jeremiah was used in warning Judah of the impending captivity, and the "pulling down" or "overthrowing" of *the* THRONE OF DAVID in the Kingdom of Judah . . . but notice the second half of the commission . . . TO BUILD AND TO PLANT! To build and to plant WHAT? Why, naturally, that which he was used in "rooting out" of Judah—the THRONE OF DAVID which God swore He would preserve forever! . . . that throne was divinely commissioned to be planted and REBUILT by the prophet Jeremiah—*during his lifetime!*[89]

The fact that Jeremiah was commissioned to overthrow the commonwealth of Judah, destroy the Davidic kingdom . . . throw down the throne of David . . . is so clear, so well known . . . then that throne of David was again set up, the seed planted, and the kingdom builded up before Jeremiah died.[90]

Many other parallels can easily be seen between Mr. Armstrong's book *The United States and British Commonwealth in Prophecy* and J. H. Allen's work, *Judah's Sceptre and Joseph's Birthright.* Unique points appear in both books such as those discussions on the descendents of the Zarah line, the ministry of Jeremiah after the fall of Jerusalem and the stone of Jacob. Furthermore, the discussion of words such as "saxon," "British," and "Dan" are the same. Also, identical verses are used with identical emphases to prove identical points. It must also be kept in mind that these issues mentioned above are part and parcel of the British-Israelite theory, which was popular long before the beginning of Mr. Armstrong's work. Finally, it is worth noting that J. H. Allen's book was first published in 1902, three decades before the founding of the Worldwide Church of God.

The Influence of Other Groups

The four theologies mentioned above are not the only ones which evidently influenced Armstrongism. Herbert W.

Armstrong severed his relationships with the Church of God (Stanberry, Missouri), but he did bring several of its unique teachings out with him. For example, the emphasis on the name "Church of God" as being the only legitimate name for the true Church of Jesus Christ is common to both. Also, the insistence that Christ was crucified on Wednesday and rose on Saturday is found in the literature of the two groups. They both condemn certain holidays as pagan and declare that true Christians should not observe them. Both organizations have published a pamphlet entitled, "Has Time Been Lost?" This pamphlet attempts to demonstrate that Saturday is the true Sabbath of God, even though there have been changes in calendars and time reckoning through the centuries. These pamphlets are identical in both the words used and the illustrations given. It is obvious that the Stanberry group has shaped some of Mr. Armstrong's thinking.

Armstrongism has also been influenced by orthodox Christianity. This, at first, may seem like a strange statement to make. However, it must be understood that Armstrongism is not orthodox. It has accepted, on the surface, some orthodox doctrines and has employed much of the terminology of orthodoxy, but the Worldwide Church of God is clearly not orthodox, since it has modified or changed nearly every major doctrinal area held by biblical Christianity. This will be demonstrated later in the book.

Summary

Herbert W. Armstrong, the founder, and Garner Ted Armstrong, the heir apparent, are the dominant personalities in the movement of the Worldwide Church of God. They have brought this group to a place of power and influence today.

Herbert Armstrong has repeatedly stated that he owes no debt to any previous religious system. Yet, it has been seen that a great many of the "new" concepts of the Worldwide Church of God are the same as those found in religious

groups established decades before Herbert Armstrong com-
menced his movement. His claim to uniqueness and authority
cannot be accepted. His theological system is definitely
eclectic.

A Summary of the Teachings of the Worldwide Church of God

It is the purpose of this chapter to give an overall view of the doctrinal system of the Worldwide Church of God. The major areas of theology will be dealt with in this summary as they are presented in the literature of this movement. Many details within each of the major doctrinal areas cannot be specifically mentioned, since this is not a comprehensive study. However, when the primary teachings are understood, the position held in secondary areas can usually be deduced.

The Doctrine of the Scriptures

Revelation and Inspiration

God used various methods of disclosing new truth to men. This He did without allowing any errors or human opinions to enter the text. The very words of the Bible were inspired by God.

> But—regardless as to the original character of various of the Bible books, letters and journals—ALMIGHTY GOD selected them as part of *His inspired Scripture!* He said, *inspiring* the Apostle Paul to tell us, *"All Scripture* is given by inspiration of God" ... if there is *one single word of the original inspired Scriptures* which is not valid, and which is *UNinspired,* then there remains no authority whatsoever for saying that ANY of the Scriptures are inspired. Either the Bible is ALL inspired—or you can have confidence in NONE of it. [1]

Authority

The Bible has real authority in men's lives today, and is, in fact *the* authority of God. As Jesus Christ, the living Word, is supreme, so the written Word is also. "That SUPREME AUTHORITY is Jesus Christ, and His written Word, the BIBLE."[2]

Canonicity

The Bible is composed of the sixty-six books of the Old and New Testaments. There are no additional books, such as the Apocrypha. The Bible is complete.

> The Bible is COMPLETE! Not one book of the Bible has been lost. Not one is missing. The books of the Bible as you find them in your King James Version constitute the complete Bible![3]

The Bible and Higher Criticism

The views of higher criticism are to be rejected. The late dates applied to many Old Testament books, such as Daniel, are erroneous. The critic's bias against supernaturalism causes him to manufacture these dates. The fragmentation of the Old Testament books by assigning several authors to one book, as in the case of Isaiah, is likewise to be rejected.[4]

Illumination

Very few see and grasp the meaning of the Scriptures. One must be in a right relationship with God, doing His will, before truth can be rightly understood. This is especially true of prophetic truth which comprises the greater part of the Bible.

> Those who do not yield to God and submit to His *way* cannot hope to understand. Only those who have been enlightened by God's Spirit—made "wise"—can hope to grasp and comprehend prophetic meanings.[5]

God's true servants alone are used to bring enlightenment concerning Scriptural truth.

> Understand that God reveals prophecy through His true servants . . . Amos 3:7: "Surely the Lord God will do nothing, but he revealeth his secret unto his servants the prophets." . . . Remember, ONLY God's true servants have come to properly understand prophecy. . . . Wherever you can find a "Work of God"

which fulfills these conditions—which keeps God's Commandments—there you will also find God revealing His secrets—which
means opening up Bible prophecies for the practical understanding of future events.[6]

Summary

Evangelical Christianity and the Worldwide Church of
God hold a very similar position in the realm of Bibliology.
Armstrongism is far sounder here than many of the theologians and churchmen who lead a great many of the large
groups in Christendom. The Worldwide Church of God holds
to verbal plenary inspiration and rejects anything which
would modify that stance. It sees revelation as complete, in
that God no longer is adding to the body of inscripturated
truth. It should be obvious, however, that its position on
illumination opens the way to theological deviations. Its position at this point resembles that of the Roman Catholic
Church, which assigns to itself the role of interpreter. By so
doing, any doctrinal aberration can be justified by explaining
that only true servants of God can understand and communicate the truth that God has revealed to them.

The Doctrine of God

The Existence of God

The existence of God is proved by the fact that the universe, which is clearly the product of power and an infinite
mind, is in existence. God is the only One who could give life
and create an orderly system governed by immutable law. He
is the only One who could design this intricate universe and
give life.[7]

> But He who did the *creating*—He who brought everything that
> exists into existence, including all else falsely called God . . . He is
> God! He is superior to all else that is called "God." He, alone, is
> GOD![8]

The Personality and Attributes of God

God is called a Father and is greater in every way than
any other beings. He has greatest authority and responsibil-

ity.[9] He is eternal, self-existent, all wise, all powerful, merciful and loving.[10] God is perfect and righteous, as His very nature and character are revealed in the Law. He is all knowing, except that He has voluntarily limited His knowledge of the salvation of men, choosing not to know who will be saved or lost.[11] God is a Spirit being, but has shape and form.

> Man is created in the shape and form of the real, living Creator God. . . . God from eternity has possessed hands, ears, eyes, arms—and feelings, emotions, reason, will. Therefore God, when He began His plan of reproducing Himself, created Adam and Eve with *His* body shape, and with a mind capable of creative thought like God's! Of course, man is now physical while God is Spirit.[12]
> God made man in the physical form and *shape* of God (Gen. 2:7), to *look* like God. But He made man out of *totally different material!* God is a Spirit," said Christ (John 4:24).[13]

The Names of God

There are many descriptive names of God in the Old Testament which reveal much of the nature and character of God. One of the primary names of God is "Yahweh." Through this name, God shows Himself to be the Eternal God who is the Self-existent One.[14] God is also known by the name "Elohim," a uni-plural noun which reveals God to be a family.

> The word *Elohim* is a uni-plural noun. It is a word like "church" or "family." There is *one* family—but *many members*. There is *one* church—but *many members*. Thus, there is one God—but *more than one member* in the Godhead, or God family!
> . . . This Father-Son relationship shows that God is a FAMILY. And the way the word *Elohim* is used in these early passages in Genesis and elsewhere certainly indicates that God is the *creating kingdom or family*.[15]

The Trinity

The Godhead is not limited to three persons. At the present time two individuals compose the Godhead, the Father and Son. However, at the future resurrection the God family will be added to, making it much more than three persons.

"*God* is a *Family*—not a trinity. God's Family will not be limited to an intractably closed circle of three. . . . *God's* Family is open!"[16]

The Father

God is called a Father because He is a Father. He is the Father of Jesus Christ and He begets men as the Sons of God.[17] He is the Father of Creation as well.[18]

The Decree of God

God does not predestine all things. There is no predestining of men to be saved or lost. Predestination refers to the call of God now, during this age to a life of training in the truths of God. Individuals can leave the calling.[19]

Summary

The Worldwide Church of God teaches many things in common with orthodox Christianity on the Godhead. Its view is that God the Father is both personal and powerful, possessing most of the attributes generally ascribed to Him by biblical Christianity. The majesty and authority of the Mighty Creator God continually find emphasis in Armstrongism. However, in several vital areas there is a departure from the orthodox position. First, the view that God is a family is at total variance with the biblical position. The denial of the Trinity puts the Worldwide Church of God outside the circle of biblical Christianity. Second, it holds that God is a Spirit, but nevertheless has Him possessing physical form and shape. This view resembles that of Swedenborgism, but doesn't go as far as Mormonism. Spirit is not a refined form of matter, but rather an immaterial substance. Third, its view that God has imposed a restriction on His own knowledge damages the attribute of omniscience.

The Doctrine of the Holy Spirit

The Personality of the Holy Spirit

The theologians have long taught that the Holy Spirit is a person. This is not true. The Holy Spirit is not a person, but rather is the power of God. It is the force or power which comes out of God and is used by Him in performing His will. A person cannot be "poured," "quenched" or "renewed." ". . . the Holy Spirit is not a person but the power God the Father uses—much as a man uses electricity."[20] God's Spirit is His mind, His power, His very essence, but it is not a distinct person as is the Father or Christ.[21]

The Procession of the Holy Spirit

The Spirit of God proceeds from both the Father and the Son.

> But the Holy Spirit is the SPIRIT that emanates *from* both the Father, and from CHRIST, and literally enters INTO us, *begetting us,* so that we may BE BORN as the VERY sons of God![22]

The Work of the Holy Spirit

God implants His Power in believers in order that He might express Himself through them. Believers, who have repented and been baptized, receive this Power of God which enables them to keep God's Law, become an heir of God, become partakers of the Divine nature, and eventually receive immortality.[23]

Summary

The denial of the personality of the Holy Spirit naturally affects this entire doctrine. The Spirit's ministries in the believer, in the unbeliever, and in the life of Christ are all greatly changed when He is viewed as a force or power from God. As a result, there is no agreement at all in this doctrinal area between biblical Christianity and Armstrongism.

The Doctrine of Christ

The Person of Christ

His Pre-existence

Christ has existed from all eternity with the Father. He is One with the Father, but He is subordinate to the Father.

> The Greek word is *Logos.* It means "Word," or "Spokesman." This is referring to the One who co-existed with the Father from eternity—who is one with the Father, yet, as He Himself said, His Father is greater than He. [24]

Before his human birth at Bethlehem, Christ was Jehovah of the Old Testament, the God of Israel. It is He who appeared to Moses, Abraham and the other Old Testament greats.

> The *meaning,* in English, is "The Eternal," . . . It is commonly supposed that *Yahveh,* or *Yahweh* . . . of the Old Testament was God the Father of Jesus Christ. This is a *flagrant error!* . . . In almost every Old Testament passage, the Lord *Yahveh*—the Eternal—is Jesus Christ. He is the God of Israel. [25]

His Incarnation

Christ the Eternal God became man. When born of the virgin Mary, He was converted to human flesh. It was *not* that God entered into a human body, but rather that He was changed into human flesh with all of its weak and sinful human nature. He was God in that He retained the character of God.

> Notice, He did not merely enter into some mortal fleshly body—the body of another. He was not separate from the flesh, as One inside the flesh . . . *it says He was made flesh!* That is, He Who had existed from eternity . . . He *was made flesh!*—converted into flesh, until He *became* flesh; and then He WAS flesh!
>
> And, being flesh—being human—He divested Himself of inherent immortality for the time being. . . . Yes, Jesus was a fleshly MAN. He was God come in human flesh. [26]
>
> Christ, one of the beings in the Godhead, had now been *changed* into flesh—still having the *personality* and *will* to do right which distinguished Him as an entity—yet now had become *human,* having HUMAN NATURE with all of its *desires, weaknesses* and *lusts*—and subject to death like any other hu-

> man ... the Satan-inspired doctrine that Jesus was *not* human, that He did *not* inherit the human nature of Adam, that He did *not* have all the normal human passions and weaknesses against which all of us have to struggle—in a word, that Jesus did *not* really come "in the flesh" as a normal human being—this is the doctrine of the Anti-Christ. ... The *only* difference between Jesus and any other human is that He was conceived of the Holy Spirit ... He, who had been God, was now changed into *human flesh* with all its weaknesses and lusts. Nevertheless, He retained in His personality the *determination,* the WILL *to obey God always.* ... Men were permitted to *worship* Jesus because He was the *personality* and *perfect will* of one who was *God*—and He exercised the *character* of God.[27]

Christ was not the Son of God in eternity past, but became the Son of God when born of the virgin.

> As a human, Jesus was the Son of God the Father. God was His only Father. Mary was His mother. He became the SON of God at his human birth.[28]

His Humanity

Christ was a human being exactly as we are human beings. He was a fleshly man, inheriting human nature from his mother. Being human, he was able to die.

> That is, as we humans are partakers of flesh and blood, Jesus Christ, also, in exactly the same manner, was partaker of flesh and blood. And why? Why, in order that he *might* DIE![29]

His Deity

Jesus is God. In nature He is equal with God the Father, though the Father is greater. He is called God, therefore, He is God. He is a member of the God Family.

> Therefore Christ's life is the life of the *Creator* God. Paul called Him "God our Saviour" (Titus 1:3). Yes, in the person of Jesus Christ, the very *Creator* became our *Saviour!*
>
> Christ is our Maker and a member of the Godhead—the God Family.[30]
>
> And so God the Father is greater than Jesus Christ (and remember I didn't say it, *Jesus Christ did!* (John 14:28) in that *this* God is the Father of *that* God we call Jesus Christ the Son.[31]

The "Kenosis"

When Christ became a man he took upon himself sinful flesh and "emptied himself of being God."[32]

His Impeccability

Christ never sinned when He was on the earth, though He could have. Since He had sinful human flesh, the very nature of man, He daily faced temptations to sin. Man can be tempted, but according to the Scripture God cannot; therefore, proving that Christ was indeed a man. If He had sinned He would have been eternally lost and unable to die as the saviour of men.

> Day and night, while on this earth, Christ must have remembered the tremendous power and glory *from all eternity* He had enjoyed with the Father—and realized it would have been possible to *sin*, to *relent* in His battle against human nature, and *become eternally lost!* The very willpower, the determination and perseverance of Jesus Christ, together with the Divine presence of the Holy Spirit of God, kept Him from falling that He could become the Saviour of the world![33]

Jesus never sinned and did not need salvation from sin, but He did need to be "born again." He is the "firstborn among many brethren" (Rom. 8:29). His being born again at his resurrection shows that we who are His brethren will be born spiritually also. He was born spiritually, that is, made a spirit being capable of entering the Kingdom of God, by means of the resurrection (Rom. 1:3, 4). He is the only one thus far to be "born again."[34]

The Work of Christ

His Death

It was necessary for Christ to die in order that the penalty of sin be paid. Man had no hope without His death. Salvation's plan was begun on the Cross, but not completed there. The shed blood of Christ in itself does not completely save men. His blood removes past sins only.

> If Jesus had been *only* human, His death could have paid the penalty for but *one* other human being who had incurred that penalty by transgression of God's spiritual law. . . . He is our Maker and therefore God; and His life which He gave was of *greater value* than the total of all human beings (John 1:1-3).[35]
>
> People have been taught falsely, that "Christ *completed* the Plan of Salvation on the Cross"—when actually it was only *begun* there. . . . The BLOOD of Christ does not finally save any man. The death of Christ merely paid the penalty of sin in our stead—it wipes the slate clean of past sins—it saves us merely from the DEATH PENALTY—it removes that which separated us from God and reconciles us to God.[36]

Christ was crucified and died on Wednesday afternoon, not on Friday.[37] For seventy-two hours Christ himself was completely dead—not just his body being dead. Christ ceased to exist for three days and three nights.

> Jesus DIED! Jesus WAS DEAD! And for three days and three nights the Second person of the Godhead—EMMANUEL—God with us—God made human flesh—was DEAD! . . .
>
> If there were no other Person in the Godhead, then the Giver of all Life was dead and all hope was at an end. If there were no FATHER in heaven while Jesus Christ lay dead—His blood in which resided HIS life, shed from His veins, given for you and for me—then all human life everywhere had come to its doom.[38]

His resurrection

After being in the grave for the full three days and three nights, Christ was raised by the Father on Saturday.[39] After His resurrection Jesus was invisible, except when, by an unexplained process, he made himself visible to men.[40] Jesus did not rise from the dead in the human body that was placed in the tomb. He was a spirit being after the resurrection.

> And the resurrected body was no longer human—it was the Christ resurrected IMMORTAL, once *again* CHANGED! . . . now by a RESURRECTION FROM THE DEAD, HE WAS AGAIN CHANGED, CONVERTED INTO IMMORTALITY.[41]

His Ascension and Present Ministry

After His resurrection, He ascended as the glorified Son of God to heaven, to the very throne of God.[42] He is now developing godly character in repentant men by means of the Power of God. His life is being lived through those who have accepted Him.[43]

Summary

The Christology of the Worldwide Church of God is difficult to comprehend entirely because of the confusion and contradiction within the system. In viewing the Person of Christ it seems that Armstrongism believes that Christ is both God and man—the biblical teaching. However, a number of statements show that its position is not that of Orthodox Christianity. First, Armstrongism actually has three Christs who have no relationship to one another, except on paper. The pre-existent Christ is said to be Jehovah the Eternal One of the Old Testament. (It should be noted that Armstrongism is not careful when dealing with the Persons of the Godhead.) At the incarnation, an entirely different person is presented. He is definitely not the God-man of the Scriptures who is truly human, and yet, who is also undiminished deity. He is not the one who veiled his pre-incarnate glory, took on the *likeness* of sinful flesh and voluntarily gave up the use of certain attributes. In Armstrongism, Christ is totally a man (having "emptied himself of being God") and only by the force of God retained the ability to reveal the will and character of God. However, it is an elementary fact of theology that giving up the attributes of deity means that he ceased to be God. This "second" Christ theoretically could have been eternally lost; a concept impossible to understand. The idea of one of the Persons of the Godhead being eternally separated from the other is incomprehensible, yet that is the position of the Worldwide Church of God.

At his resurrection, He was then converted into a spirit Son of God. He did not retain the human body or nature, so this is a "third" Christ. Thus, when putting the pieces together, the Worldwide Church of God has a pre-incarnate Christ who is the Great God Jehovah, who then changed into a human being with sinful flesh, but having no deity. He was then changed into a spirit Son of God, something He was not before becoming a man. There is simply no logical or biblical way that these "Christs" can be the same person.

There are other major problems in the Christology of the Worldwide Church of God. Christ, as a human being, can only be rightly understood in the light of its position on the nature of man—that he is mortal, material and having no distinct entity as soul or spirit. As it will be seen later, this position colors the thinking in a great many areas. In this system, then, Christ could never become a God-man in the biblical sense.

The position of Armstrongism on the person of Christ raises some questions on such things as the equality of the Father and Son, the place of God the Father in the Old Testament, and the problem of imputed sin in relationship to Christ.

On the work of Christ the position of Armstrongism is more understandable, but not more biblical. Christ's death paid for the repentant, baptized sinner's past sins. Then, by Christ living through him, the sinner is eventually brought to sonship. This area will be dealt with later under the doctrine of salvation.

Christ died and ceased to exist for three days according to the theology of Armstrongism. It holds that the Second Person of the Godhead actually ceased to exist. How can God be God, with such attributes as immutability, eternality, and unity, and still cease to exist? Among other things, the "God Family" ("Elohim") would have gone out of existence for three days since there was no plurality left in the Godhead.

The resurrection of Christ was spiritual. Nothing is said about the old human body of Christ, as to what happened to it. Christ, according to Armstrongism, received immortality at this time. This raises many more questions, such as, if Christ as a person did not previously have immortality, which is an attribute of God, then how could he be God? If

He did have it, then how could He cease to exist? Before the incarnation and resurrection, what was the relationship of the two Persons in the Godhead, if it were not Father-Son? How can the Father be qualitatively greater than the Son? Some of these matters will be studied in more detail in the next chapter. The whole Christology of the Worldwide Church of God is replete with contradictory positions as well as outright error. This most critical of doctrinal areas shows Armstrongism found wanting.

The Doctrine of Angels
Holy Angels

God created an order of spirit beings known as angels. These were created before mankind was created to populate the earth. These holy, or obedient, angels minister to men who are heirs of salvation and immortality.[44] These angelic beings did not follow Lucifer when he fell.

Satan

Satan was originally created as Lucifer, the shining one. He was a great cherub who had a place of rulership over other angelic beings. He is described as a glorious creature in Ezekiel 28. He desired to be like God Himself and fell, taking one-third of the angels in heaven with him in his rebellion. This fall and the resulting battle in the spirit world caused the earth to become chaotic, "waste and void." The Devil is called the "god of this world." This does not mean, however, that he is in control, because God controls everything. However, Satan does deceive men, especially in the area of religion.[45]

During the millennial kingdom, Satan will be bound for the entire thousand-year period. He will then be released, rebel, and finally be cast into the Lake of Fire to suffer forever. Jesus said that the Lake of Fire was prepared specifically for the devil and his angels, and since they are spirit beings they will be punished in fire forever without being consumed.[46]

The Demons

Demon is the name given to the wicked angels that followed Satan in disobedience. They are under Satan's authority. Today they are active in deceiving men through religion, and Spiritism in particular.[47] Their fate is the same as that of Satan.

Summary

Generally, the statements of the Worldwide Church of God in the area of angelology coincide with those of many evangelical Christians. There are differences of opinion among scholars on issues such as the "gap theory," the binding of Satan, and the interpretation of Isaiah 14, Ezekiel 28, and Jude 6. The stated beliefs of Armstrongism in the doctrine of angelology are to be found in the various segments of orthodox Christianity.

The Doctrine of Man

The Origin of Man

Adam, the first human being, was created by a direct act of God. The account of man's creation in Genesis is to be taken literally—God made man out of the dust of the ground. God created Adam as a perfect physical specimen.[48] The creation of man took place approximately six thousand years ago.[49]

The Fall of Man

God was responsible for the Fall because He planned and permitted it to happen. To say otherwise would mean that Satan was more powerful than God and able to thwart His plans.

> Now if Satan did *not* succeed in thwarting God's will, wrecking God's perfect and complete Creation, then the only alternative is to say it all happened *according* to God's will—*exactly as God Himself originally planned!* . . . Either Satan got in there *against*

> God's will, and in so doing proved himself mightier and more
> cunning than God—or else God Himself planned and permitted it
> all![50]

God planned and permitted the Fall by creating man with an
evil nature that would resist and rebel against His Law.

> God knew that Adam would react to a given situation in the same
> general manner as every other human being would react to that
> same situation. As Adam "went" so all mankind would "go."
> God *designed* human nature to be vain, jealous, lustful, greedy,
> and antagonistic to God. . . . So Adam sinned and hid himself
> from God—precisely conforming to God's specifications.[51]

The Nature of Man

Contrary to the teachings of most churches, man was not
created with an immortal soul—an entity that exists after the
body dies. Man is mortal as the animals are mortal and he
does not possess immortality. "The life of *man* and the life of
animals is the same! MORTAL life."[52] When man was created
out of the dust by God, the breath of life was breathed into
his nostrils and at that time man became a living soul.

> Man *became* a living SOUL; that is what man IS—a *soul.* Notice
> there is no mention that man has a soul, but that man *is* a
> soul! . . . *there is not one single expression in the entire New
> Testament of your Bible where the word "soul" can have any-
> thing whatsoever to do with immortality, eternal life . . . or any-
> thing other than mortal, temporary life!* . . . Soul in the Greek,
> comes from psuche, which means "breath." . . . Thus, it corre-
> sponds *exactly* to the Hebrew *nephesh* which means the tempo-
> rary life of animals![53]

Man, therefore, is a mortal being, subject to death. Immortality is pictured in the Bible as something to be sought after,
not something already possessed.

> In each case, immortality is something that is *brought to light,*
> that must be *obtained,* that God ONLY has, and in no case is
> something man already possesses![54]

The Destiny of Man

It is commonly taught that at death man goes to heaven,
"hell," or some type of purgatory. This is not true. Because

he is mortal, man at death ceases to be conscious—he "sleeps" in the grave. "Death is the *absence* of life, the cessation of life—not the continuation of life under different circumstances."[55]

The individuals who have been converted during this life and have kept the commandments of God will become spirit sons of God at their resurrection. They receive immortality and divinity at this time.

> ... that through the resurrection of those BEGOTTEN BY THE HOLY SPIRIT OF GOD during this mortal life, this MORTAL then *puts on* IMMORTALITY, and we, like the very God Himself, become IMMORTAL, INCORRUPTIBLE, actually literally BORN of God's Spirit INTO the very GOD FAMILY.[56]
> ... we develop spiritually ready to be finally BORN OF GOD—by a resurrection, or instantaneous conversion from mortal to immortal—from human to divine. . . .[57]

The individual who lived his life in blindness to the truth will be given an opportunity at his resurrection to hear and obey. This is not a "second chance," since the individual never had a first one.

> Those who *have never had* an opportunity to learn about God's Word and His laws, who never even heard the only name whereby man must be saved (Acts 4:12), must have that opportunity! Religious hobbyists, arguers, scoffers, and bigoted antagonists will oftentimes accuse the Great Creator for this masterful plan of offering a so-called "second chance"! ... But IS this a *second* chance? When, pray tell, did these millions of wretched, hapless, disillusioned and illiterate souls have a "FIRST" chance? They never did, but they will.[58]

However, should these then refuse to obey the truth, they will be annihilated and cease to exist forever.

> The "wages of sin is death" (Romans 6:23) and the *death,* which is the *absence* of life, is for ALL ETERNITY. It is eternal *punishment* by remaining DEAD for all eternity—not remaining *alive* and being tortured in a fictitious, burning *hell-fire!*[59]

Summary

The position of the Worldwide Church of God is generally the same as Seventh-day Adventism. As it will be seen in the following chapter, this view of the nature of man is built upon a misunderstanding and misrepresentation of biblical concepts and words. The doctrine of man's individual destiny rests on the concept of his nature, and thus if one is erroneous then the other will be also. Man is more than mortal flesh on the same level as animals. Man is composed of immaterial as well as material elements. Armstrongism shares its position on anthropology with other cult groups.

The Doctrine of Sin

The Definition of Sin

I John 3:4 gives the biblical definition of sin. Sin is breaking any or all of the Ten Commandments.

> What is sin? Despite the contradictory ideas and generalizations of organized religious denominations, *your Bible* clearly states: "Sin is the transgression of the law" (I John 3:4). . . . Sin is *breaking God's spiritual law*—the TEN COMMANDMENTS. That is *definitely* and *specifically* what sin is![60]

The Sin Nature

The Apostle Paul describes inner conflict and struggle in his personal life and shows this to be his human nature. Human nature can hold men captive in sin. This is the "law of sin and death" that resists the "law of the mind," which is the Ten Commandments.[61]

Man was created with a carnal nature that naturally resists God and His Law.

> God *designed* human nature to be vain, jealous, lustful, greedy, and antagonistic to God—so that when man would learn to *control* his carnal nature, eternal and Godly character could be developed.[62]

Personal Sin

Even after being converted, a person will commit sin. However, if, with a repentant heart attitude, he confesses that sin, he will be forgiven. However, deliberate, premeditated sin, if continued in, will mean the loss of God's Spirit and eternal ruin.[63]

Summary

In some areas of this doctrine of hamartiology, the Worldwide Church of God has not been precise in defining terms, such as the concept of imputed sin. However, its doctrine does stress the utter seriousness of sin and stresses the need to be free from it in order to have a right relationship with God. Perhaps the most significant factor in this doctrinal area is the definition given for sin. It is important because it affects very definitely the issue of salvation. Armstrongism again follows the lead of Seventh-day Adventism by using I John 3:4 as its one and only definition of sin. Sin, according to both groups, is a breaking of the Ten Commandments. A lengthy refutation is not called for here. It is sufficient to note that this text is simply not speaking about the decalogue. John is pointedly declaring that all sin is iniquity, wickedness or lawlessness. Sin is said to be a disregard for law, without any reference to the decalogue. The concept of "law" is far more extensive than simply the Ten Commandments. Law is used of other standards besides the decalogue. Armstrongism consistently makes the error in its teaching of assuming that every appearance in the Bible of "law" or "commandment" is a reference to the Ten Commandments. A good translation would be, "Sin is lawlessness." To build a complicated superstructure on this verse is not legitimate, since the text does not teach what Armstrongism claims it does.

The Doctrine of Salvation

The Definition of Salvation

Salvation is a process which begins in this life and is completed at the resurrection. Salvation is not the present possession of any man, since it is future. When a person is finally saved, he will be changed completely in every way.

SALVATION means being BORN into GOD'S KINGDOM, changed from a flesh-and-blood mortal HUMAN, *to* a Spirit-composed, life-inherent IMMORTAL son of God the Father—the Father of the divine Family.[64]

Repentance and Faith

God begins the salvation process by causing a man to see that his way of living is wrong and in need of a change. The first steps in the process are those of repentance and faith (Mark 1:15). Repentance is accomplished by sincere and earnest prayer to God regarding sin, confession, turning away from one's evil ways and beginning to live according to God's Commandments.[65] Faith is absolutely necessary in the salvation process. A person is saved by faith, not by works.

Then are we saved by works *instead* of faith? No. NEVER! We are saved by FAITH! But faith functions *with our work* and BY WORKS our FAITH IS MADE PERFECT! That is LIVING FAITH! ... Yes, faith *establishes* the Law! By keeping it, is faith made perfect! ... A LIVING FAITH—the only kind that will SAVE—is an *active* faith—one that TRUSTS GOD to make it possible to OBEY HIM—to live the true Christian life—TO KEEP His blessed Commandments.[66]

True repentance and faith will cause one to live according to God's commandments.

REPENTANCE and FAITH. Those are the two things *we must do!* Repentance is toward God. Faith is toward Christ. Repentance means to *quit sinning*, and sin is the transgression of God's spiritual LAW—so repentance means to begin living according to God's Commandments! And Jesus said, "believe the GOSPEL." And the GOSPEL is the GOOD NEWS of the Kingdom of God—which means GOVERNMENT of God, and government means obedience to LAWS, in this case God's laws, which express the will of God—government by the WILL OF GOD, no longer by human self-will![67]

Baptism in Salvation

Water baptism is a required part of the way of salvation. It was commanded by Christ as part of the divine Commission, and is, therefore, a required condition for salvation. The water itself does not save a person, but rather it is a matter of obedience to a command of God. All who are able must be baptized in order to be saved, or else disobedience causes the loss of salvation. In rare cases, such as the thief on the cross, God makes allowances, since circumstances cannot be controlled. This is possible since water itself does not save. The receiving of the Holy Spirit depends on water baptism and is essential for salvation.

> Now water baptism is a required CONDITION to receiving the Holy Spirit . . . GOD COMMANDS WATER BAPTISM. The water baptism *is not the thing that saves us.* While it is commanded "for the remission of sins," yet it is merely symbolic of that which remits our sins—the DEATH OF CHRIST . . . God *commands* water baptism; and for one who is able to either defy the command and refuse, or neglect . . . certainly would be an act of disobedience which would impose the PENALTY of sin, and cause loss of salvation.[68]

Baptism, to be valid, must be by immersion and should be administered by a true servant of God.

The Conversion Experience

When a person is converted, he is changed. This change, which is sometimes referred to as "accepting Christ," occurs when he receives the Holy Spirit at the time of water baptism. When the Holy Spirit is received, the person is begotten as a son.

> We are then merely begotten, spiritually—comparing to an unborn human babe still in its mother womb—not yet really BORN. We then become merely HEIRS of the Kingdom—not yet inheritors . . . A PERSON IS NOT EVEN BEGOTTEN OF GOD UNLESS HE IS CHRIST'S (I John 5:12). AND HE IS NOT CHRIST'S UNLESS HE HAS RECEIVED THE HOLY SPIRIT (Romans 8:9). One is not even converted—spiritually begotten—not even STARTED on the way to final salvation, unless and until he RECEIVES THE HOLY SPIRIT FROM GOD![69]

So this conversion experience comes about when one accepts Christ and receives the Holy Spirit.

The New Birth

Contrary to the teachings and claims of many, no person has yet been born again, except for Jesus Himself. The term "born again" does not apply to the conversion experience and has nothing to do with the removing of sin. The conversion experience is the time when a person is begotten. The Greek word γεννάω refers to an actual birth and not to the conception which occurs much earlier. The birth takes place at the resurrection. At this time the "begotten" individual is born—born a spirit being even as Christ (I John 3:2).

> When we are converted, our sins forgiven, we receive the Holy Spirit, we are then BEGOTTEN of God—*not yet* BORN of God. If this has taken place—if we have been converted, *begotten*, we are truly, already SONS OF GOD (I John 3:2) but what we SHALL be, when BORN of God, does not yet appear—for then WE SHALL BE LIKE HIM—like Christ in His resurrected glorified body![70]
>
> Even AS Christ was BORN AGAIN, born of God, by His resurrection, even so WE—*the brethren*—shall be BORN AGAIN as sons of God, through the RESURRECTION of the dead, BY His Spirit that dwells in us![71]

Important Concepts in Salvation

Justification

A person is justified at the time of conversion. Justification is being saved and forgiven of sins that are past, upon repentance and faith in Christ. The death of Christ accomplished our justification.[72]

Sanctification

Sanctification means being set apart for a holy use or purpose. It is a process that leads to ultimate salvation, which is the change from mortal to immortality, from material to spiritual, from human to divine.[73]

Redemption

Redemption is the great *spiritual* creation of God. Redemption is not the repairing of the damage done by the Fall, nor the restoring of man to that original position held by Adam. Redemption is the creating process of God whereby He will make men *holy, perfect, spiritual* characters.[74]

Righteousness

We must be righteous to be accepted of God. If we obey God's commandments we clothe ourselves with God's kind of righteousness and are acceptable to God. God does not impute to men something they do not have. Christ, by HIS power in us, makes us righteous.

> There are those who say: it is IMPOSSIBLE for us to live righteously, so Christ lived a righteous life IN OUR STEAD, and if you just believe, God IMPUTES Christ's righteousness to you. . . . their false argument means you are free to go on deliberately SINNING, but God PRETENDS you are righteous, by a sort of hocus-pocus of transferring *Jesus'* righteousness to you.[75]

Law and Grace

Law and grace are not mutually exclusive. In fact, it is only by obedience to the law, after receiving the benefits of Christ's sacrifice, that one is under grace.

> The law has a penalty—DEATH. It claims the life of the one who transgresses it. The law has power to take the life of the transgressor. It therefore is more powerful than the sinner—and is OVER the sinner, holding a claim on his life. It is the SINNER who is UNDER the Law. But when the sinner REPENTS of his transgression, and accepts the sacrifice of Christ as payment of the *penalty* of the law, then he is PARDONED—UNDER GRACE—the law no longer stands OVER him, claiming his life. Those who are still sinning are still UNDER the Law! And those who, through repentance, obedience and FAITH have turned from disobedience and are, through faith, KEEPING the Law, are the *only* ones who are UNDER GRACE.[76]

Eternal Security

A converted person remains in his position as a begotten son of God as long as he has the Holy Spirit. By sinning and remaining unrepentant he can lose the Spirit and thus his salvation. We are converted persons "are now *begotten* sons of God and, if we don't abort ourselves in this growth process, we'll later become *born* sons of God."[77] There is, therefore, the possibility that one who was converted can again be lost.

Summary

The Worldwide Church of God teaches that salvation is a process. This process begins when the two conditions of repentance and faith are met. Following the meeting of these conditions it becomes absolutely necessary for the individual to be baptized. The conversion experience itself then occurs, and it is at this time that the Holy Spirit comes and the person is begotten of God. The experience of conversion is sometimes referred to as accepting Christ as Saviour. The process of growth (sanctification) begins. The salvation process will be completed at the resurrection when the new birth actually takes place; meaning that the individual becomes an immortal spirit being.

It is not the purpose of this chapter to refute the teachings of Armstrongism. However, several observations should be made. It should be observed that it is in this doctrine of soteriology that the semantic juggling becomes most obvious. As it was noted in the first chapter, the redefining of terms is a characteristic common to all cults. This enables them to use orthodox terminology and yet not disturb their own system. Oftentimes entirely different concepts and definitions are assigned to words that have been otherwise understood. In this section, for example, the terms "new birth" and "justification" take on meanings that are totally different than those held by Orthodoxy. Also, it should be noted that partial truths are given in the defining of such concepts as sanctification and baptism.

One final observation should be made concerning the subject of salvation. Herbert Armstrong vehemently denies that he teaches a works salvation,[78] but his denial is forcefully contradicted by his own writings and those of his staff. Keeping the Ten Commandments and baptism by immersion are very definitely requirements for getting and keeping salvation. "Faith" is so altered that it ends up meaning to keep the law (see the quotation under "Repentance and Faith").

"Grace" is tampered with so badly that one is only under grace when the law is being kept (see the quotation under "Law and Grace"). Salvation in Armstrongism is contingent upon keeping God's Ten Commandments all through life. Therefore, there is not nor could be any security for the believer. Armstrongism, in the doctrine of salvation, is simply the old Galatianism with a new twist.

The Doctrine of the Church

The Definition of the Church

The Church began on the Day of Pentecost, A.D. 31, and is composed of begotten sons of God. It is not some politically organized denomination, but rather it is a spiritual organism. One cannot join the Church; only God can put a person in it by the means of His Spirit.

> The true Church is the collective body of individuals, called out from the ways of this present world, who have *totally* surrendered themselves to the rule of God, and who, through the Holy Spirit, become the begotten sons of God (Rom. 8:9). Jesus has purchased *this Church* by shedding His own blood for it.[79]

The Name of the Church

One of the identifying marks of the true Church is that it does not deny the name of God (Rev. 3:8). While others might name their churches after men, doctrines or church government, the true Church will name itself after God.

> The number *twelve* is used by God throughout His Word as the number of *organized beginnings*.
> So it is certainly significant that the NAME of the true Church should be stated exactly twelve places in the New Testament! The true Church is not named after any man . . . it is God's Church—*so it is named after God!*
> . . . we are THE CHURCH OF GOD—so named *twelve* places in your Bible![80]

The Universal Church

The Church is not a building that people walk into, nor is it an organization for doing good. The Church is the Body of

Christ: Jesus Christ is the head and the Church of God is the Body.[81] The Church cannot be joined, because only God adds people to the Body.

> . . . it is God who *puts one into* His Church. And HOW? By His Spirit! When God bestows within one His Holy Spirit, that puts the believer into the Church.
>
> The CHURCH is composed of those who are the begotten CHILDREN of God—of the FATHER of the divine Family. One *becomes* a begotten SON of God upon receiving within him the Holy Spirit of God.[82]

The Local Church

Although the Church is not simply an organization, God has given structure to it. The local church has individuals who are gifted and placed over the Work of God.

> Putting all New Testament passages together, the ADMINISTRA-TIVE offices, in order of rank and authority under Christ, were: 1st apostles; 2nd, evangelists (in the New Testament, prophets did not have administrative offices) . . . pastors; preaching elders; and local non-preaching elders and teachers. There also were deacons and deaconesses, appointed to take care of physical duties.[83]

The true Church of God, therefore, is a spiritual organism but it is organized.

Baptism is an ordinance given to the Church. Many of the counterfeit churches do not properly use this ordinance. Baptism is by immersion only of those who are mature—usually over twenty-one years of age.[84]

The Lord's Supper has been given to the Church as an ordinance to remember the death of Christ. The Lord's Supper is the New Testament Passover and is a continuation of the old Passover, only with different elements. The Lord's Supper should be celebrated once a year on the anniversary of the event of the Lord's death (the 14th of Abib). Some have assumed that the New Testament reference to the "breaking of bread" refers to the Lord's Supper. This is not the case. The "breaking of bread" never indicates the Lord's Supper, but simply the eating of meals together.[85]

The Church Today

After A.D. 69 the true Church was scattered. It completed two nineteen-year cycles of ministry in the world, from A.D. 31 to A.D. 69. The true Church became impotent, absorbed pagan elements and all but disappeared. However, before the Second Coming of Christ, God has allotted two more nineteen-year cycles to His Church in order to carry the Gospel to the world (1934 to 1972). In 1934, God raised up Herbert W. Armstrong to carry out this task of publishing the gospel to the world. The Worldwide Church of God is God's true Church today.

> And there is only ONE CHURCH on earth today which understands and is PROCLAIMING that exact order of events, doing the WORK of God in preaching His message to the world as a last witness, really "feeding" the true flock with stronger and stronger spiritual meat so they may be literally BORN of God by a resurrection from the dead when Christ returns! . . . What you are now reading is part of the inspired, God-directed work of that Church—the very WORK of God which He first did through Jesus' human body, and is now doing through the instrumentalities in His Church. . . . This is God's Church—and as God intended, it is named "The Church of God!"[86]

Summary

Much of the terminology used in ecclesiology has an orthodox ring to it. There is talk of being placed into the Body, and of Christ being the Head. However, once again the changing of terms and concepts has made the teachings quite different. If the Holy Spirit is merely a force and the Body is the "Church of God," then the concept of Spirit baptism takes on entirely new meaning.

In the writings of the Worldwide Church of God the focal point is on the universal church, since it is the entire "World Tomorrow" movement that is significant to them. The local church is a factor to be sure, but it is not emphasized.

In Armstrongism, there is a heavy Old Testament aroma pervading the atmosphere of the New Testament Church. The

Law is still clearly in force. The Lord's Supper is simply a continuation of the Passover which is to be kept just once a year. Admittedly among orthodox churches there are different views on the frequency of the celebration of the Lord's Supper, but the Worldwide Church of God rigidly holds a once a year Passover celebration as an article of faith and views anything else as disobedience. This position has the flavor of Old Testament legalism. Also, in spite of the fact that Armstrongism believes that the Church started on the Day of Pentecost, it holds the view that the church is built upon the Old Testament prophets as well as the New Testament apostles (Eph. 2:20). Again there are differences of opinion within orthodoxy. It does seem preferable to interpret the Ephesians 2:20 passage as referring to New Testament prophets since the absence of the article before "prophets" would link them grammatically with the "apostles."[87] However, the Worldwide Church of God views the Old Testament prophets as part of the church's foundation because it contends that many Old Testament prophecies were never written for Israel at all.[88] This position is essential to the British-Israelite view of this group since these prophecies are said to be written to the lost tribes of Manasseh and Ephraim (the United States and the British Commonwealth).

Two items especially draw the attention of one who studies the ecclesiology of Armstrongism, aside from the tremendous claims for the movement itself. Of particular interest is the significance attached to the name of the church, and also the emphasis on the two nineteen-year time cycles.

Great stress is placed on the name "Church of God" as being an identifying mark of the true Church, but in the New Testament, Christ and the apostles gave no instructions to the Church to assume any particular name. The Worldwide Church of God points to twelve references where "Church of God" is found. However, the words "church" or "churches" appear over one hundred times in a variety of contexts, but the Scriptures fail to single that phrase out as the key name. Believers were designated by a number of expressions, such as "that way," "Brethren" is used over 350 times and often of church members.[89] It would seem just as legitimate for any church with "brethren" in the title to claim that its name identifies it as God's true Church. If a specific identifying name had been selected by the Lord, certainly it would have been given by Him or his apostles in some declarative statement. It must be concluded that the name itself does not mark any group out as being special to God. However, what they do with the truth of God does mark them out.

> In view of this Biblical evidence, it seems clear that the New Testament endorses no explicit name for the corporate body of believers. Neither Christ nor the disciples, not even John, the last of the apostles, ever clearly announced one. Obviously the teaching, rather than the name, stood out as important.[90]

It is also of interest to realize that the Church of God (Seventh-day) of Salem, West Virginia used this argument to prove it was God's true church. This was several years before the Worldwide Church of God (then the Radio Church of God) began its movement. It will be remembered that Herbert Armstrong separated from this group before he started his own movement. Evidently he took some of their argumentation along with him when he left and incorporated it into the Worldwide Church of God.[91]

Herbert Armstrong believes that the nineteen-year time cycles are significant to his work. The nineteen-year lunisolar cycle is selected to show how God often works. For example, Christ began to preach and teach his followers one hundred time cycles before God began teaching Herbert W. Armstrong (A.D. 27 to A.D. 1927). This nineteen-year time cycle was devised by Meton, a fifth century B.C. Athenian astronomer. He noted that 235 lunar months corresponded with nineteen solar years. Astronomers have since recognized a slight error in Meton's system.[92]

Now where Herbert W. Armstrong got the idea that this is

somehow significant to the work of God is difficult to ascertain. According to Herbert Armstrong, the year 1972 should have ended the work of God and brought in the events of the last days (1934 to 1972 completes the two nineteen-year time cycles). This has caused Armstrong some prophetic problems which now force him to say that "the whole question of chronology is in confusion."[93] However, this issue and others like it cannot be dismissed in such a manner. Very clear and definite predictions have been made by Mr. Armstrong and others through the years and one cleverly written article cannot be allowed to set these aside. Those within the movement as well as those outside of it accepted these pronouncements as specific predictions (whether they believed them or not is not the point). These "prophecies" cannot be banished in the name of human error and fallibility or the confusion of the age. The predictions were made authoritatively and with the seeming sanction of the Scripture. Some key examples are given.

(1) A devastating drought to hit the United States.

> But the indications of prophecy are that this drought will be even more devastating than he foresees, and that it will strike *sooner* than *1975*—probably between 1965 and 1972! This will be the very *beginning* as Jesus said, of the Great Tribulations.[94]

(2) Martyrdom ahead for the professing Christians in America and Britain.

> Yes, millions of lukewarm inactive professing Christians will suffer MARTYRDOM—and that *before* the anticipated push-button leisure-year of 1975 dawns upon us! You'll read of this martyrdom—the Great Tribulation—in Matt. 24:9-10, 21-22.[95]

(3) The resurrection of the Roman empire by 1972.

> So, mark carefully the *time element!* "In the days of these kings"—in the days of these ten nations or groups of nations that shall, *within the decade,* now, IN OUR TIME, resurrect briefly the Roman Empire.[96]

It should be noted that the emphasis of this statement is on the time that is involved. This revival of the Roman empire is to take place within the decade. The publication date of this pamphlet is 1962, which clearly indicates that the outside limit for the resurrection of the Roman Empire is 1972.

(4) Destruction shortly of the peoples of America and Britain.

> It (Lev. 26) was a WARNING to those of Moses' day—but its final fulfillment, as we shall see, has taken place—and is *now taking place—in our time.* And, through the duality fulfillment, typical of so many prophecies, it is also a WARNING to the American and British peoples of impending events to occur within the next five to eight years! And this WARNING *has been* thundered in great power to these very Birthright Israelites during the past 34 years.[97]

The publication date for this book was 1967, which places the fulfillment of this prophecy somewhere between 1972 and 1975.

(5) America to experience major droughts, famines and epidemics by 1971, 72.

> Now, other prophecies reveal, we are to have soon (probably in about four years) such drought, and famine, that disease epidemics will follow taking millions of lives. . . . Well, we have been getting foretastes of that! That condition is coming! And I do not mean in 400 years—nor in 40 years—but in the very next FOUR or FIVE![98]

The publication date of 1967 makes these predictions already out of date. They should have been fulfilled in 1971 or 1972. The following prediction was made in the same book.

(6) Intense punishment for the United States by 1972-74.

> You need to look at the prophecies of Jesus, of Jeremiah, of Isaiah, and others, describing how *much more* INTENSE is to be the punishment God is going to lay on the British and American people in five to seven more years![99]

(7) The gospel of Christ will be preached until 1972.

> God gave the Apostolic Church *just two* nineteen-year cycles to carry the gospel to the Old World. He opened a DOOR to the apostle Paul *at the beginning of the second nineteen-year cycle* by which the gospel went to Europe (Acts 16:9; II Cor. 2:12-13). So

> now, just before the second coming of Jesus Christ, God has given His Church—THIS CHURCH—*just* *two* nineteen-year cycles in which to carry the gospel to the world! The first cycle *passed.* Then God suddenly opened the door for the second cycle in January 1953, and the gospel is now going to all the world![100]

Several points need to be made concerning this predictive statement. First, it was not given by Herbert Armstrong himself, but by Herman Hoeh, one of the leaders in the Worldwide Church of God. It is, however, an accurate reproduction of Mr. Armstrong's own teaching. Second, the time cycles began in 1934 and should have ended in 1972. Third, this prediction clearly indicates that Christ's coming is connected with the completion of the time cycles. Fourth, the time cycles are rigid and not elastic, and therefore do not permit the kind of stretching that is currently being undertaken by the Worldwide Church of God.

Any unbiased reading of these predictions causes one to sense the authoritative prophetic nature of these words. It is such authoritative predictions that has drawn many into the Worldwide Church of God.

The Scriptures do not regard lightly those who would speak for God. Jeremiah 28:9 and Deuteronomy 18:20-22 declare that true prophets would be accredited as such by the fact that their messages came to fulfillment. If a single prediction was made that failed to come to pass, that prophet was a false one and definitely not from God even though he spoke in God's name.

Herbert Armstrong denies that he is a prophet, but denying the label does not negate the fact that he has attempted to function as a prophet. Specific predictions were made and that in the name of the Lord, and now that the time for fulfillments has past or is very near, there is an attempt to modify and soften these predictions. However, Scripture has made itself clear about the status of those who find themselves with unfulfilled prophecies on their hands. This situation of Herbert Armstrong and the Worldwide Church of God certainly reminds one of William Miller and the predictions of the early Adventist movement.

It has been necessary to examine briefly these two positions of Armstrongism at this point in the study because they will not be touched on later.

The ecclesiology of Armstrongism is definitely dominated by its claim to be the only valid channel in the world today for God's message. This claim is one reason why a study of Armstrongism is necessary.

The Doctrine of Future Things
The Second Coming of Christ

Jesus Christ is going to return to this world a second time, but this time as a conquering king. He is going to come down literally and stand upon the Mount of Olives outside the city of Jerusalem. He will then rule in power and glory.

> In many other prophecies it is recorded that the second coming of Jesus Christ to this earth—the time of Christ's literal bodily return to this earth shall occur at the *time* of the last trump! . . . this same Jesus is coming again in almighty POWER and GLORY. He is coming as a world RULER—as KING of all kings—as LORD of all lords, to rule *all nations,* and to enforce the way to PEACE![101]

As He descends to the earth, the begotten sons of God, both dead and living, will rise to meet Him in the clouds and then descend with Him to the Mount of Olives.

> Just *as* He is returning (I Thessalonians 4:14-17) the dead in Christ—those who have received and been led by God's Holy Spirit (Romans 8:11, 14), will rise in a gigantic RESURRECTION, made IMMORTAL—including all the prophets of old . . . and together with those resurrected, shall rise to meet the descending glorified Christ (I Thessalonians 4:17) in the clouds in the air. They shall be with Him, where He is, and stand *with Him,* therefore, that very same day, on the Mount of Olives (Zechariah 14:4 and 5).[102]

Immediately at Christ's coming will occur the Battle of Armageddon, when the last Satanically inspired resistance will be eliminated.

> Simultaneously, at the very Presence, or coming, of Christ and all the holy angels, the *seven last plagues* of God's Terrible Day of WRATH shall be poured out on the remnants. . . . As the Battle of this Great Day of the Lord comes to its fateful end, with the armies assembled at ARMAGEDDON destroyed, and as the final plague of the seven last PLAGUES is poured out, the military "Fuehrer" and the "False Prophet" . . . will be taken together, and cast alive into a "lake of fire burning with brimstone."[103]

The Rapture

Many Protestant Churches falsely teach that before the terrible events of the last days, Christ is going to rapture secretly His saints out of the world. This view is a product of recent times and was not a doctrine of the original Church. Jesus never taught a secret rapture, but instead warned His followers to be alert for the Tribulation. There is simply no place in the New Testament Scriptures for a secret rapture. Those who hold to such a view are in grave danger, since they are looking for the wrong events and will not be prepared when the last days come suddenly.

> But, the clear statement was that Jesus' ultimate return to this earth would be in exactly the *same manner* in which He left. Jesus Christ went straight up into the atmosphere of this earth and disappeared into the clouds as He made His ascent into heaven. Jesus Christ is going to return in precisely the same way— straight down out of the clouds of the air to the solid ground of this earth. Jesus is *not* going to pause in mid-air to rapture His saints and then return to heaven. If this were so, these angels *lied.*[104]

The Tribulation

The Tribulation that Jesus spoke about in Matthew 24 will last about three and one-half years. In Revelation 6, there are various "seals" described. The first five are Satan's wrath upon this earth. Mankind is right now experiencing the first four, though they will grow still greater in intensity. The fifth seal *is* the Great Tribulation period.

> We have truly entered the days of which Jesus Christ spoke in Matthew 24. These same days are mentioned in Revelation 6. . . .

> These first five seals are *Satan's wrath* upon this earth. These events are caused by man *disobeying God* and following the ways of Satan the Devil to his own hurt and destruction.[105]
>
> NOTICE that! Here is the GREAT TRIBULATION! And this 5th seal pictures it as a time of *martyrdom of saints*—of truly converted, begotten children of GOD![106]

World War III will begin at the start of the Tribulation and Germany will head the "Revived Roman Empire" (the "king of the north").

The Day of the Lord

The Day of the Lord follows the Tribulation period. Many have mistakenly equated the two, but they are in reality distinct from one another. The Tribulation is the time of Satan's wrath while the Day of the Lord is the time of God's wrath (the Trumpets and the Vials). Immediately after the Tribulation the sixth seal is broken and great signs and wonders are seen in the heavens which will cause great anxiety and fear among men. These great signs signal the beginning of the Day of the Lord.

> This is the time of God's wrath. This is the time of GOD'S PLAGUES sent upon the sinners of this world. . . . This is the time of the PLAGUES God shall send—but this is not the Great Tribulation, as men have supposed!
>
> . . . it is vital to understand the distinction between the Great Tribulation and the Day of the Eternal.
>
> The Great Tribulation is not the wrath of God—just the opposite. *This is* the wrath of SATAN THE DEVIL.[107]

All persons who repent during these times will be protected along with all of God's begotten sons.

> These all shall receive God's Holy Spirit—be then begotten as children of God. And who shall then, at last—having endured the Great Tribulation—having seen God's terrifying warning SIGNS—repent and put their lives in God's hand, shall come under God's divine protection. NO PLAGUE will touch them (Psalm 91:1-11).[108]

The Day of the Lord leads directly into the Second Coming of Christ.

The Millennium

After Christ successfully destroys the wicked armies at the Battle of Armageddon, He will set up his worldwide kingdom which will last for one thousand years. Peace will come to this earth at last.

> And Christ will rule over and judge all nations, UNTIL they beat their swords into plowshares, their weapons of destruction into implements of peaceful PRODUCTION.
>
> When, at last God *takes over*—puts down Satan, and the WAYS of Satan's world . . . then the NEW World—The WORLD TOMORROW shall reap what it then sows—PEACE, HAPPINESS, PROSPERITY, HEALTH, ABUNDANT, INTERESTING LIVING, OVERFLOWING JOY! It will be a Utopia beyond man's fondest or wildest dreams.[109]

During this millennium of peace and prosperity, Satan will be bound.[110] Some mortals will survive the previous days of judgment and will live in the kingdom and be given the chance to become the sons of God.[111] In fact, in this age God really begins in earnest to save people.[112] This kingdom of Christ will be perfect in every way, from just and righteous government to full prosperity and productivity in agriculture throughout the earth.[113] There will be a few rebellious individuals at the beginning and end of the millennium, but they will be firmly dealt with by Christ.[114]

The Future Judgments

Believer's Judgment

Begotten sons of God will receive their rewards at Christ's Second coming. Those who have faithfully worked for God will receive the reward of rulership with Christ in His kingdom. The greater the faithfulness, the greater will be the rulership. "He will then assign the positions in His government—the "reward"—to those who already "are saved."[115]

The "Sheep and Goats" Judgment

The "sheep and goats" judgment will continue throughout the entire thousand years of Christ's reign on earth. Those mortals who are converted during this period are His "sheep," and those mortals who live in the kingdom and rebel are the "goats" and they will be judged.[116]

The Great White Throne Judgment

The people of all the ages who were spiritually blinded to the truth of God will be the subjects of this judgment. It is not a judgment of condemnation, but rather one of opportunity. These will be given a period of time in order to hear the truth and then they have the opportunity to accept or reject it. It will be the first chance for all of them to see this truth, and therefore it is definitely not a "second chance." This judgment takes place after the thousand-year reign of Christ.

> Therefore it is the vast blinded majority, who never really had a chance to accept God's way of life, who are resurrected! . . . It is the great white throne judgment! Even the worst of the sinners who never had a chance will be in this resurrection, for even the inhabitants of Sodom will be there! . . . Isaiah 65:20 indicates those resurrected at that time will live for a hundred years. God is indeed a just God (Deut. 32:4) and all will have their chance to be saved![117]

Judgment of the Wicked

Immediately following the Great White Throne judgment, all the wicked will be raised. These are those who heard and rejected God's truth. They will be eternally punished—annihilated.[118]

The Resurrections

Aside from Christ's resurrection, there are three resurrections. The first will be for all of the begotten sons of God at which time they will be born again. This occurs at Christ's Second coming. The second resurrection will take place at the end of the millennium and will involve all people who had never heard or understood the truth of God. These will be given a period of time to respond to the true Gospel of

Christ. The third and final judgment will be of the wicked, who will be raised and then cut off forever.[119]

Summary and Conclusion

The eschatology of Armstrongism is detailed and involved. The general order of future events as given in this system is as follows: (1) a continual intensifying of the first four seals at the present time; (2) the fifth seal will be broken, which is the Great Tribulation; (3) the sixth seal will be broken and there will be great wonders in the heavens; (4) the Day of the Lord comes; (5) Christ's Second coming, the first resurrection and the Battle of Armageddon occurs; (6) Christ will then reign for one thousand years on the earth; (7) the second resurrection takes place; (8) the third resurrection occurs; and (9) the new heavens and earth are brought in.

In reading the prophetic literature of the Worldwide Church of God it becomes obvious that the British-Israelite theory held by this group underlies much of the interpretation. Many Old Testament passages are directly applied to the United States and Britain. This subject will be taken up in the following chapter.

The student of the prophetic Scriptures is also impressed with the way prophetic phrases and passages are misused. Matthew 24, Revelation, Ezekiel 33–39 and other sections are badly mistreated. In some cases the interpretation is unnaturally literal, while on other occasions a passage is allegorized so badly it loses meaning.

There are some evident contradictions in the eschatology of Armstrongism. For example, it is emphasized throughout the literature of Armstrongism that their true church will be protected by God during the times of trouble; yet, the three and one-half years of Tribulation is explained to be a time of great martyrdom. It is interesting as well to the student of Armstrongism that there is such great emphasis on the bodily ascension, return, and rule of Christ; yet Christ is said to be merely a spirit being who can materialize in some unknown way. The emphasis of the Worldwide Church of God is certainly different from that of the Scriptures.

It has not been within the scope of this chapter to deal with all the details of this system of eschatology. Some things like heaven, hell, the mark of the beast, and other points of discussion could not be handled in this section. An entire study could easily be devoted to the eschatology of the Worldwide Church of God.

Some Special Teachings

In concluding this survey of the teachings of the Worldwide Church of God, several distinctive teachings are included in order to get a more complete picture. These are not critical doctrinal areas, but they are of practical importance in the propaganda and ministry of this movement. Many are first attracted to the Worldwide Church of God by its presentations on these less important subjects, and then indoctrinated later in the essential, basic teachings of this movement.

Armstrongism and Holidays

A great deal of time is spent in the literature of the Worldwide Church of God in showing that Christmas, Easter, New Year's, Halloween, Valentine's Day, birthdays and others are of pagan origin. Every year *The Plain Truth* (or *Tomorrow's World*) takes time to deal with these holidays, and for a definite purpose. To most who observe these various holidays, any pagan background has nothing to do with their celebration of them, and thus little or no importance is attached to their supposed origins. The feeling is that every man decides for himself about the keeping of days (Rom. 14:5). However, Armstrongism uses these holidays effectively in its attempt to show that it is the true Church of God. If it can show, for example, that December 25th was a pagan holiday that the Church adopted and "Christianized," it then feels it has laid a foundation on which to charge the church with adopting pagan ideas in doctrine. The reasoning is this: if the false church adopted the pagan day of December 25th, then why is it hard to see that it has adopted the pagan ideas of the immortality of the soul and the trinity. Therefore, it can be observed that while most think that this emphasis of the Worldwide Church of God is simply religious enthusiasm gone awry, it actually is one of the most potent tools used to establish its claim of doctrinal purity and genuineness.

Armstrongism and Government

The emphasis of the Worldwide Church of God is on the world of tomorrow and not the world of today. Since this present order is Satan's system, true Christians will not attempt to improve Satan's world. The Christian is to regard himself as a paying guest of the country he is in, and this is all. He is to pay taxes and obey laws (as long as they don't violate God's laws), but is not to vote, join the military or join anything that would promote and improve this system of Satan.[120]

Armstrongism and Medicine

Physicians and medicine are contrary to God's will, according to the Worldwide Church of God. It further believes that using medicine is another evidence of ancient paganism in modern life. It is only God who heals and there isn't a cure in a carload of medicine.[121] This view is a part of Armstrongism's emphasis on the dietary laws and the eating of natural foods.

Summary of the Chapter

The purpose of this chapter has been to summarize the various teachings of the Worldwide Church of God under the standard headings of theology. In some, such as angelology and bibliology, its doctrinal position is quite close to the orthodox position. In others, such as soteriology and Christology, its teachings clearly classify it as a cult.

The attention of the study will now be directed to the analysis of specific teachings of the Worldwide Church of God and a refutation of these views.

A Refutation of
Some Major Doctrinal Errors
of the Worldwide Church of God

In viewing the total spectrum of the beliefs of the World-wide Church of God, there are several critical areas where error is found. These areas, of course, are not the totality of doctrinal deviation in this system, but they are the key ones. They are important because they affect almost every major area of theology and most of the subdivisions of these major divisions.

It will be the purpose of this chapter to analyze the following subjects: the British-Israelite theory; the Persons of the Godhead; the nature and destiny of man; the Person of Christ; the concept of the new birth; and the Law in its relation to salvation.

The British-Israelite Theory in Armstrongism

The theory of British-Israelism is the foundational philosophy on which the Worldwide Church of God rests. This theory teaches that the ten tribes, called Israel, are today the Anglo-Saxon people. It was formulated by an Englishman, Richard Brothers, around 1800. All the basic tenets of British-Israelism, found in every British-Israelite work, are to be found in Armstrongism as well. Yet in spite of this fact, Herbert Armstrong claims that he has found this truth which is the key that unlocks the prophetic Scriptures.[1] A brief summary of this theory will be given which will expose the

key points of it. The summary will be based on the book by
Herbert Armstrong, *The United States and British Commonwealth in Prophecy.*

A Summary of British-Israelism in Armstrongism

The theory begins at the Abrahamic covenant and develops from there. It is said that in the Abrahamic covenant
physical blessings are promised as well as spiritual ones. In
Genesis 17:1-5, Abraham was informed that the material
blessings of the land were to be received by many nations.
God gave Abraham additional information after the successful passing of the test with Isaac in Genesis 22. Here God told
Abraham that "your race shall possess the gates of its enemies." These "gates" are explained.

> A gate is a narrow passage of entrance or exit. When speaking
> nationally, a "gate" would be such a pass as the Panama Canal,
> the Suez Canal, the Strait of Gibralter.[2]

So Abraham's descendants would eventually possess strategic
locations. This is concluded when Genesis 28:13, 14 is added
and declared to teach that these nations of Israel would eventually spread around the world.

> The original Hebrew for "spread abroad" means "to break forth."
> This promise places no *limit* on how far east, west, north and
> south Jacob's descendants should spread. Thus it indicates they
> would spread around the earth.[3]

Later Jacob was told that God would make a company of
nations out of him (Gen. 35:9-12).

The Abrahamic covenant, therefore, is used as the launch-
ing pad for further speculation, after supposedly proving that
part of the blessings were material and were slated for more
than one nation. The two steps in the reasoning have to do
with the birthright of Genesis 48 and 49, and the necessity to
distinguish between "Jews" and "Israel."

In Genesis 48 and 49 is recorded the deathbed testament
of aged Jacob. Jacob promised to Judah that the line of kings
would come from him and would not depart until the Mes-

siah came. Christ came, of David's line, and brought great spiritual blessing to the whole world. However, the birthright went to Joseph, in the person of his sons Ephraim and Manasseh. These, who would later lead the nation of Israel, received the material blessings promised Abraham through the birthright. The tribe of Judah ("Jews") were not given the great national material promises.

> The Birthright Promise *did not* pass on to the Jews! But the Sceptre—the promise of CHRIST and of GRACE *was* passed on to the Jews! ... The astonishing and *vital* fact that MANY have overlooked is "the Birthright is JOSEPH's." And, as we shall see later, neither Joseph nor his descendants were Jews! ... This knowledge about the BIRTHRIGHT is the pivot of this entire truth which will prove THE KEY to the understanding of all PROPHECY![4]

The distinction made between Israel and Judah (the Jews) is of vital importance as well.

> We want to impress, here, that Israel and Judah are not two names for the same nation. They were, *and still are,* and shall be till the second coming of Christ, TWO SEPARATE NATIONS. The "House of Judah" ALWAYS means "Jew."[5]
>
> The terms "House of Israel," or "all Israel," when the meaning is national, or the terms "Jacob," or "Rachel," or "Ephraim," or "House of Joseph," or "Samaria," often used in the Bible in prophecy, RELATE TO THE TEN-TRIBED BIRTHRIGHT PEOPLE, NOT TO THE JEWS. This is a KEY, and a Master Key, to Bible understanding![6]

The Davidic covenant is the next subject of discussion as this theory progresses along. It is said that a proper understanding of the Covenant with David is absolutely necessary. God promised that David's throne would never cease even for the length of one generation.

> Almighty God made an absolutely binding ... covenant with David, UNCONDITIONALLY guaranteeing that there should never be a single generation from that time forward when there would not be a descendant of David, in UNBROKEN DYNASTY, sitting on David's throne, ruling over children of Israel! It was the promise of continuous unbroken DYNASTY—all generations *forever*—that was guaranteed.[7]

The line down to Zedekiah is clearly there, but at that point it seems to end. However, the line must continue if God's promise is to be fulfilled.

At this point in presenting the theory, it is necessary for Mr. Armstrong to pause and explain what happened to the northern tribes at the hands of Assyria in 721 B.C. He explains that when the Northern Kingdom was conquered, it was completely driven out of the land and lost from view. This statement is based on II Kings 17:18. They then became the "Ten Lost Tribes." He claims that it was predicted that they would lose their identity (Deut. 32:26), their religion (Isa. 8:17), their language (Isa. 28:11), their name (Isa. 62:2) as well as their land.[8] They were driven out of Canaan never to return.

> In 721-718 B.C. ISRAEL began to be "carried away out of their land to Assyria" (II Kings 17:23). They were soon all removed—completely. "There was none left but the tribe of Judah only" (II Kings 17:18). JUDAH, *only*, remained.
> Those who *returned* to Palestine to rebuild the temple and restore worship 70 years after Judah's captivity, were ALL of the House of Judah—*all Jews*—ALL of those whom Nebuchadnezzar had carried away.[9]

British-Israelite Armstrongism next locates the northern tribes in Britain. By combining Jeremiah 3:11, 12, 18 and Hosea 11:8, 10, the conclusion is reached that the "lost" ten tribes went to the northwest to a place in the sea—which is said to be Britain.

> Hence, Israel of TODAY—Israel of the day of Jeremiah's "planting" of David's throne—is located specifically as NORTHWEST of Jerusalem, and IN THE SEA![10]

One proof given to support this is the supposed Hebrew names of Britain. The proof is as follows.

> The Hebrew for "man" is *iysh*, or *ish*. In English, the ending "ish" means "*of* or *belonging to*" . . . in the original Hebrew language vowels were never given in the spelling. So, omitting the vowel "e" from *berith*, but retaining the "i" in its Anglicized form to preserve the "y" sound, we have the Anglicized Hebrew word for covenant, *brith*.

> The Hebrews, however, never pronounced their "h's". . . . So the Hebrew word for "covenant" would be pronounced, in its Anglicized form as *brit*.
> And the word for "covenant man," . . . would, therefore be simply, "BRIT-ISH." And so, is it mere coincidence that the true covenant people today are called the "BRITISH"?[11]

A similar twisting trail is followed to equate "Isaac" with "Saxons."

The Tribe of Dan is brought forward as proof also. Combining the "waymarks" of Jeremiah 31:21 and changing Genesis 49:17 to read "serpent's tail," it is stated that in its travels from Canaan to Britain this tribe left its mark as is seen by the names of certain places. Any names that have "dn" in them are listed as identifying names, proving that the Tribe of Dan passed that way. A long list is given, but a few will suffice to illustrate.

> Then, in either ancient or later geography, we find these waymarks: *Dan*-au, the *Dan*-inn, the *Dan*-aster, the *Dan*-dari, . . . the Eri-*don*, down to the *Danes*. "Denmark" means "Dan's Mark."[12]

After "successfully" getting the northern tribes to Britain, the problem remains as to how the unbroken line of David is to continue after the fall of Jerusalem in 586 B.C. British-Israelism, and Armstrongism, hold that Jeremiah was called to fulfill a twofold commission (Jer. 1:9). He was called to two nations—Israel as well as Judah.[13] However, his commission was to pull down David's throne in the Kingdom of Judah and to rebuild and plant it in the House of Israel.[14] The theory contends that after the destruction of Jerusalem, Jeremiah went to Egypt along with the rest of the rebels of Johanan, taking with them the daughters of Zedekiah. It is said that Isaiah 37:32 foretold Jeremiah's escape to the north (Britain). Jeremiah took the daughters of Zedekiah with him to Ireland. One of these girls, by the name of Tea-Tephi, married Herremon and established the Davidic dynasty there. Later the throne was "overturned" and "planted" in Scotland and then, finally, it came to England where today the same dynasty continues.[15] Thus, the line remains unbroken in England (Ephraim) and will continue until the return of Christ to establish his kingdom. The United States is considered to be Manasseh, fulfilling the promise that Manasseh would be a great nation (Gen. 48:19).

The Basic Tenets of Armstrong's British-Israelism

In the above summary it was necessary to leave out a number of the details and "proofs" of this theory. However, what was given represents a fairly accurate summary of the position. This theory has certain points which must be considered, but when they are answered, the entire system collapses, and that is especially significant when it is remembered that the British-Israelite theory is the cornerstone of the Worldwide Church of God. In an attempt to deal with the refutation in an orderly manner, this writer has concluded that there are four basic tenets to Armstrong's British-Israelism. These four will be discussed in the following order: (1) the supposed distinction between "Jews" and "Israel," (2) the concept of the birthright, (3) the proposition that the northern tribes were lost, and (4) the proper understanding of the perpetuity of David's throne.

The Supposed Distinction Between "Jews" and "Israel"

The rigid distinction between "Jew" and "Israelite" is a key to the position of Armstrongism. However, it is in error in two very basic ways. First, it is a fallacy to presuppose that the term "Jew" stands for the bodily descendants of the tribe of Judah, and second, the actual biblical usage of the terms in question will not allow for such a distinction as made by Armstrongism.

The term "Jew" signifies those of all tribes who were considered subjects of the kingdom of Judah. Obviously the basic geographical area of the tribe of Judah is involved, but there were thousands of people from all tribes living in that region, as will be seen further on in this study. In discussing the word "Jew," *The Jewish Encyclopedia* comments that the word is a gentilic adjective from the proper name "Judah," seemingly never applied to members of the tribe, however, but to members of the nationality inhabiting the south of Palestine.[16]

In both biblical and secular usage, the term "Jew" has far broader meaning than the physical descendants of Judah. In discussing this word, von Rad states,

> The fall of the northern kingdom and the deportation of 722 introduced a new change in the significance and use of the name Israel. . . . Israel is now adopted by the southern kingdom and it is used again for the whole of God's people as a spiritual designation which transcends such political titles as the house of Judah or the province of Judah.[17]
>
> After the return from exile the people is even more exclusively restricted to the province of Judah, and all those who live in Palestine outside this province are non-Israelites. It is thus quite natural that the name which derives from the territory . . . which originally denotes an inhabitant of the kingdom or province of Judah should come to be used more generally for a member of the people of Israel.[18]

The two terms can include both groups. For example, Asa and Jehoshaphat, kings of Judah, are called "Kings of Israel" (II Chron. 28:19; 21:2). These descendants of David were in the only legitimate line that could rule the people of God.

This switching of terms is particularly noticeable in the postexilic books. David Baron brings together the following statistics.

> Anglo-Israelites say they were only the exiles from the southern kingdom of Judah, and call them "Jews." I have already shown this to be a fallacy, but I might add the significant fact that in the Book of Ezra this remnant is only called eight times by the name "Jews," and no less than *forty* times by the name "Israel." In the Book of Nehemiah they are called "Jews" *eleven* times, and "Israel" twenty-two times. As to those who remained behind in the one hundred and twenty-seven provinces of the Persian empire, which included all the territories of ancient Assyria, Anglo-Israelites would say they were of the kingdom of "Israel"; but in the Book of Esther, where we get a vivid glimpse of them at a period subsequent to the partial restoration under Zerubbabel and Joshua, they are called forty-five times by the name of "Jews," and not once by the name "Israel"!

In the New Testament the same people who are called "Jews" one hundred and seventy-four times are also called "Israel" no fewer than seventy-five times. Anglo-Israelism asserts that a "Jew" is only a descendant of Judah, and is not an "Israelite"; but Paul says more than once: "I am a man which am a *Jew*." Yet he says: "For I also am an Israelite." "Are they Israelites? so am I" (Acts xxi.3; Rom. xi.1; 2 Cor. xi.22; Phil. iii.5) . . . Devout Anna was a "Jewess" in Jerusalem, yet she was "of the tribe of Aser."[19]

Other Scriptures reveal the same thing (e.g., Ezra 6:17, 8:35; Zech. 1:19; 8:13; 10:6; James 1:1; Acts 2:22-24). These biblical facts absolutely overwhelm the assertions of Armstrong's British-Israelism. The distinction made by Armstrongism is vital to its system, in order to have two distinct and separate groups of God's people functioning under different aspects of the Abrahamic covenant, but the Scriptures do not permit these rigid distinctions as Baron demonstrated. There is some validity to the distinction between these terms while the kingdom was divided, but even then it wasn't as rigid as Armstrong would hope.

> But both Old and New Testaments use the terms interchangeably, except where the distinction is being made between the northern and southern monarchies during their political existence. And not too much care is given even in this case. The claim cannot be strictly defended that the appellation Israel was not applied to Judah till after the destruction of Samaria.[20]

This basic tenet of Armstrong's British-Israelism fails to stand even under a brief examination, showing that such distinctions are extremely superficial. It has not defined "Jew" properly and it has been arbitrary in narrowing the meaning of both terms.

The Concept of the Birthright

It is the contention of Armstrongism that the birthright promise and prophecy made Ephraim and Manasseh greater than the other tribes. It is also claimed that the birthright was the material blessing of the Abrahamic covenant and the sceptre represented the spiritual. Armstrongism is wrong on both counts.

First, it is not true that the birthright made Ephraim and his brother, Manasseh, greater than the others. It simply placed them on the same level as the other sons of Jacob. Joseph was the one who was exalted, not his sons. Joseph is the one who received the double portion. His sons were blessed in that they received a portion and status equal to that of the rest of Jacob's sons. The portion of Manasseh was equal to that of Asher, for example.

Second, it is incorrect to dissect the Abrahamic covenant in the manner done by Armstrongism. It is true that the covenant contained material and spiritual blessings, but the assigning of all material blessings to the birthright and all spiritual blessings to the sceptre is manifestly artificial. The sceptre included a very material land, for example. In like manner, the birthright had some spiritual aspects to it as well. The spiritual aspect of the birthright was important to the Patriarchs. As the head of the family, the firstborn (before the Aaronic priesthood was established) became the priest for the family. Esau, a man devoted to the material only, is severely condemned in the Book of Hebrews for his treatment of the birthright. His carnal mind did not really grasp the spiritual value of the birthright.

The birthright promise cannot be taken biblically to be God's guarantee that the Anglo-saxon people would rise to great power and wealth. Such theorizing is based on an unwarranted and artificial distinction.

The "Lost" Ten Tribes of the North

Another essential plank in Armstrong's British-Israelite platform is that the ten tribes of the northern kingdom were completely and totally removed from the land and disappeared from view. These tribes not only lost their land, but also their religion, identity, language and name. Furthermore, it is held that they never returned to the land of Canaan. Armstrongism's position is summed up.

> By "lost" Armstrong does not mean merely politically defunct;
> he means nationally absent. The system requires more than just
> the lostness of the political entity called Israel; it requires the
> relocation of the people—all of them.[21]

Therefore, to establish its position, Armstrongism must prove
two things: that all the inhabitants of the ten tribes were
removed from the land and thus became "lost"; and that
they stayed intact, but never returned to the land of Canaan.
This must be held in order to get Israel out of Canaan and
move them to Britain as a group. British-Israelism cannot
afford to have members of the ten tribes remaining in the
land, as this would sabotage its claim that the Anglo-Saxons
are the *true* Israelites.

In addressing ourselves to the first issue, it is not difficult
to prove that the Assyrian invasion of 721 B.C. neither completely depopulated the Northern Kingdom, nor removed
members of these tribes from all of Canaan. It can be shown
that there were thousands of northerners living in the Southern Kingdom. Also the Scriptures inform us that only part of
the people from the northern tribes were deported by the
Assyrians in 721 B.C.

The historical books of Kings and Chronicles bear witness
to several emigrations from the north. After the death of
Solomon, the United Kingdom became divided with ten
tribes forming a northern kingdom. However, at the time of
the division in 931 B.C., there were those from these northern tribes who elected to remain under the Davidic king.
I Kings 12:23 speaks of Judah, Benjamin and "the remnant of
the people." which is an obvious reference to those of the ten
tribes dwelling in the south. II Chronicles 11:14-16 adds
additional light on this same period. Here it is recorded that
those of the tribe of Levi, living in the north, moved to the
Southern Kingdom of Judah. It also states that those "out of
all the tribes of Israel" who earnestly desired to seek the
Lord came to the south.

In the year 897 B.C., during the reign of Asa, the righteous king of Judah, another large influx of people came down from the north. In response to a mighty working of God, II Chronicles 15:9 records that "they fell to him (Asa) out of Israel in abundance." Ephraim, Manasseh and Simeon are specifically mentioned, and the other tribes are implied.[22]

The Northern Kingdom fell to Assyria for the final time in 721 B.C. and the peoples of the northern tribes were deported. Yet several years later, in 715 B.C., Hezekiah invited the Israelites of the north to come and join in a Passover celebration. II Chronicles 30:10 states that messengers went "from city to city through the country of Ephraim and Manasseh, even unto Zebulun." The response to Hezekiah's invitation was not favorable, but some from the tribes of Asher, Manasseh, and Zebulun did come (II Chron. 30:11). This account certainly reveals that there were many members of these tribes left in the land.

Approximately one hundred years after the fall of the Northern Kingdom another revival was experienced by the Southern Kingdom. Almost a century after the deportation of the north, II Chronicles 34:9 informs us that Manasseh, Ephraim and the "remnant of Israel" participated in this revival along with Judah, Benjamin, and Levi. It is particularly significant that these two tribes of Ephraim and Manasseh are mentioned specifically, since they are the key tribes in British-Israelite thinking.

These passages indicate that there was an identifiable remnant from the northern tribes in the south, before and after the fall of Samaria in 721 B.C. The last two references cited also make it clear that these tribes were also distinguishable in the northern part of the land for at least one hundred years after the Assyrian conquest. Armstrongism bases its assumption that all Israel was removed from the land on just one passage of Scripture (II Kings 17:18-24). It is absolutely necessary for Armstrongism to hold to such a position if it is to develop its theory.

Besides the clear passages given above, there are several

other lines of evidence that refute the contention that all
Israel was removed (the contention based on II Kings 17).
First, "all" does not necessarily mean every individual. "All
Israel" often is looking at the nation generally and not neces-
sarily at each individual member of the nation. In some cases,
the numerical minority is called "all Israel."

> "Israel," even in national context, does not always mean the
> nation as a whole. In II Samuel 10:17 David gathered "all Israel"
> to cross the Jordan into the region where two and a half tribes are
> pictured as dwelling. As a matter of fact it was not a gathering of
> the total population, but of soldiers for a military campaign
> against the Syrians. Then the next year he sends "all Israel" into
> the same region (II Sam. 11:1), . . . So "all Israel" is away on a
> military expedition while the "rest of the people (II Sam. 12:28)
> are later gathered and taken to Rabbah to help Joab complete his
> campaign. . . . Similarly, Absalom and "all the elders of Israel"
> (II Sam. 17:4) are advised by Hushai to gather "all Israel" (v. 11)
> as though none of Israel were with David. And in verse 24 "all the
> men of Israel" are listed as the following of David. . . . In II Samuel
> 24:2-9 the numbering of "all Israel" proves to be only a military
> census; . . .[23]

So to base the depopulation of the north on the word "all" is
highly tenuous.

A second line of evidence to prove that the Assyrian
deportation did not remove all the people of the north is
found in the historical texts of Assyria. These texts state that
many inhabitants were left and that foreigners were brought
in to mix with them. Sargon's claims are recorded.

> I beseiged and conquered Samaria (Sa-me-ri-na), led away as
> booty 27,290 inhabitants of it. I formed from among them a
> contingent of 50 chariots and made remaining (inhabitants) as-
> sume their (social) positions.[24]
>
> At the beginning (of my rule) . . . the city of the Samarians I
> (beseiged and conquered . . .) who let me achieve my vic-
> tory . . . carried off prisoners (27,290 of the people who dwelt in
> it; from among them I equipped 50 chariots for my royal army
> units . . . the city of Samaria) I restored and made it more habit-
> able than before. (I brought into it) people of the countries con-
> quered by my own hands. (My official I set over them as district-
> governor and) imposed upon them tribute as on an Assyrian
> city . . . I made to mix with each other; . . .[25]

The purpose of deportations by the Assyrians was not to transport entire populations, but rather to mix populations together in order to counteract unified action against their government. Deportations only removed the elite from the land—those individuals who might be in a position to cause trouble for the Assyrians if they were left. The Babylonians continued this Assyrian policy of deportation. They removed the elite from the land and left those of little importance. II Kings 24:14 speaks of the captivity of Judah and brings out these two points. Nebuchadnezzar left "the poorest sort of the people in the land" and took the wealthy, skilled and mighty with him. This was evidently the policy of Assyria as well. The deportations did not depopulate the land. This is a mortal blow to the British-Israelite theory of Armstrongism which requires that every person be removed.[26] Deportations, therefore, were not designed to remove every individual, but rather to cripple the nation's ability to function as a nation.[27]

There is another line of proof which reveals that Israel was never completely deported and hence was never "lost." In the New Testament the twelve tribes are in evidence. Anna, the prophetess, was from the tribe of Asher (Luke 2:36). James wrote to the twelve tribes which were dispersed, but evidently not lost (James 1:1). Paul spoke of the twelve tribes who were serving God night and day (Acts 26:6, 7). The Lord Jesus seemed to be recognizing the existence of the twelve tribes in Canaan when he sent his disciples to "the lost sheep of the house of Israel" (Matt. 10). These disciples were expressly commanded to confine their activities to the land. They were forbidden to go to the Samaritans or to the Gentiles. Jesus evidently realized that all twelve tribes were there in the land.

One final area of evidence has to do with the exiles who returned to the land after the Babylonian captivity. The Northern and Southern kingdoms were defeated and deported, but by two different nations, Assyria and Babylon. However, Babylonia succeeded Assyria and the territory which it ruled was essentially the same. II Kings 17:6 tells where the Northern Kingdom was taken: "In Halah and in Habor by the river Gozan, and in the cities of the Medes." Concerning the Southern Kingdom, the Scripture simply states that it was taken "to Babylon" (e.g., Dan. 1 and II Kings 24). Here the prophet, Ezekiel, ministered to these from the Southern Kingdom (Ezek. 1:1-3). Ezekiel was told by the Lord to minister to the "House of Israel" (Ezek. 3:1-5). If this refers to members of the Northern Kingdom also, then there was a mingling of the two exiled groups.[28] It is possible, therefore, that even in captivity there was a merging together of the two kingdoms. This is substantiated by noting who it was that returned after the captivity was over.

The tribes of Judah and Benjamin were the leaders of the return (Ezra 1:5). The tribal distinctions at this time are not as easily recognized and those returning do so according to family and not tribe.

> They are no longer counted after their tribal origin, but in families and after the cities to which they originally belonged, which, for the most part, are not easy to identify; hence it is difficult to say how many belonged to "Judah" and how many to "Israel"— but that there were a good many in this company of those who belonged to the northern kingdom of the Ten Tribes, is incidently brought out by the mention of two hundred and twenty-three men of Ai and Bethel alone. Now, Bethel was the very centre of the ancient idolatrous worship instituted by Jeroboam, and, though on the boundary of Benjamin, belonged to "Ephraim."[29]

Ezra 7:7 records that "there went up some of the children of Israel." At the dedication of the temple, a sin offering was made for all of the twelve tribes (Ezra 6:17). Later another burnt offering was made by those who had come out of the captivity for all the twelve tribes of Israel (Ezra 8:35). These returned exiles certainly seemed to consider themselves as representatives of the whole nation. Furthermore, Zechariah was sent by God as a prophet to this returned remnant. He addressed his messages to Judah and Israel (Zech. 1:19; 8:13; 10:6). Again, it is well to keep in mind that the exiles were called by both names, "Jews" and "Israel."

> . . . after the Babylonian captivity, from which the Jews returned, Ezra records that the remnant were called by the name Jews (eight times), and by the name Israel, forty times. Nehemiah records eleven times that they were Jews, and proceeds to describe them as Israel, twenty-two times.[30]

In view of the preceding argumentation from the Scripture, itself, it must be concluded that this idea, so basic to Armstrongism, that the ten tribes were lost, is in error. The northern tribes were never totally removed from the north; they were continually in existence under the banner of Judah in the south; and some of them did return to the land after the captivity. The ten northern tribes merged with the tribes of the south under Judah's standard. They were called Jews, but they represented all twelve tribes of Israel.

> The biblical record carefully studied, and the Assyrian record agree that the Samarian deportation was of the military, political and industrial aristocracy. "Israel" as the national administration was deported and replaced by a leadership loyal to Assyria. The evidence from the Bible is of a remaining and continuing Israelite population. The testimony of the archaelogists is in agreement. The Jewish nation at the beginning of the inter-testament period was a twelve-tribed nation. The localized ministry of Jesus was to the "lost sheep of the house of Israel." The unreliable testimony from apocryphal literature is an insufficient argument to the contrary.
>
> It is Scripturally and historically unjustified to speak of Israel as being lost in the sense of being nationally intact but unidentified. Scripture and history show that the northern kingdom did not suffer the kind of lostness that will permit Armstrongism to be true.[31]

Disproving this essential claim in the British-Israelism of the Worldwide Church of God virtually destroys the entire theory. This is true because the "key" to this theory is the discovery of the ten "lost" tribes. If they were never lost, then there is no need to find them and build an elaborate system to get them to England. However, before the discussion is closed, one other factor must be dealt with.

The perpetuity of David's throne

The Worldwide Church of God finds it necessary to take the throne of David to England in order to fulfill God's covenant promise to David that his seed would forever rule. Armstrongism, along with all British-Israelites, teach that this means that there must be an unbroken succession somewhere or else God's promise fails.

God never told David that his seed would rule in the manner suggested by Armstrongism. In fact, chastisement was foreseen in the covenant itself, and was confirmed later by the prophet, Hosea (Hos. 3:4). God did promise David that his royal seed would be preserved, but not that there would be no interruption in the actual rule. The Davidic covenant was fulfilled in Jesus Christ, the true Son of David, the legitimate heir to the throne.

> This leads us to an important conclusion: the line which was to fulfill the promise of the eternal throne and eternal kingdom over Israel was preserved by God through the lineage which in fact did not sit on the throne at all, from Nathan down to Christ. It is, then, not necessary for the line to be unbroken as to actual conduct of the kingdom, but it is rather that the lineage, royal prerogative, and right to the throne be preserved and *never lost*, even in sin, captivity, and dispersion. It is not necessary, then, for continuous political government to be in effect, *it is necessary that the line be not lost.*
>
> All conservatives agree that the line is not lost. It came to its fulfillment in Christ. In the destruction of Jerusalem, the genealogies were destroyed and it would be impossible for Jews of today to trace their lineage back to the line of David. Accordingly, in the wisdom of God, the proof that Christ was of the line of David has been preserved, but at the same time the evidence has been destroyed for any future contenders for the honor.[32]

The genealogies of Matthew and Luke do not reveal the transference of the Davidic line to Ireland or England. They do reveal that the line of David ended in Christ.

Armstrongism misses the point when it states that David's line could not be broken for even one generation. It fails to see that the covenant is God's guarantee that David's lineage would be unbroken. Hosea 3:4, 5 anticipated that there would not be unbroken succession of kings in the Davidic line, but nevertheless affirms the eternal nature of the covenant. It anticipates that the covenant would be fulfilled in spite of an interruption in the actual ruling. After the years of exile were over and no king had been on Israel's throne, Zechariah still anticipated the coming of Messiah, the king to rule (Zech. 6, 14). There is even the suggestion from David, himself, that disobedience to God could cause a break in the succession of kings on that throne that had been given to him forever (I Kings 2:4; I Chron. 28:4, 7, 8).

Armstrongism further fails to recognize the place that Christ has as the One who has and will ultimately fulfill the covenant. According to its theory, Christ would have had to journey to England if he had wanted to claim His throne at the first coming. One wonders how John the Baptist and Christ, Himself, could have offered the messianic kingdom to Israel when it was already in England.

In connection with its teaching concerning David's throne, the Worldwide Church of God gives to Jeremiah, the prophet, a significant role. Jeremiah is said to have had a dual ministry of "overturning" and "planting." This is interpreted to mean that he removed David's throne in Canaan and established it in England. He accomplished this by taking a daughter of Zedekiah from Egypt, where the remnant had fled, and bringing her to England. There she married one of the descendants of the ten tribes. His ancestors had arrived in the British Isles centuries before and were of the "zarah" line (Gen. 38:27-30).

Besides the fact that much of this is built on Irish legend, there are a number of other fallacies to this theory. First, and certainly highly significant, is the fact that the sacred record is silent on what took place after the remnant of Judah, under Johanan, fled to Egypt. It is true that Jeremiah and the daughters of Zedekiah were part of that remnant, but there is no record of any travels after the arrival in Egypt. Tradition says that Jeremiah died in Egypt.

Second, Jeremiah's ministry of "overthrowing" and "planting" was simply envisioning the negative and positive aspects of his ministry. He thundered judgments against many nations besides Judah (e.g., 25:12-38), and he spoke of blessing and a golden age to come (e.g., 23:3-8). To interpret Jeremiah's ministry as tearing down the throne of David in Judah and setting it up in the House of Israel located in the British Isles is a classic example of eisegesis.

Third, and very important, the line of David did not go through Zedekiah. Zedekiah was not the legitimate king of Judah, since Jehoiachin and his sons were still alive in Babylon when Zedekiah was ruling in Jerusalem. Zedekiah, Jehoiachin's uncle, was placed on the throne by Nebuchadnezzar. Furthermore, Zedekiah is not included in the genealogy of Christ, the fulfiller of the Davidic covenant.

Fourth, it is also important to note that Zedekiah had no sons, since Nebuchadnezzar had them all killed in the destruction of 586 B.C. (II Kings 25:7). He had no living sons and the line is never passed along through daughters. Only the king's sons had a legal right to the throne. Even if Zedekiah's daughters had travelled to the British Isles, they still could not have established the legitimate Davidic dynasty.

Fifth, there is no historical record anywhere that Jeremiah and any daughter of Zedekiah journeyed to England, taking the throne with them. Neither secular sources, nor the Scriptures, validate this contention of the British-Israelites. Armstrongism takes verses from Ezekiel, Jeremiah, and Isaiah to plot the route to England. The verses used, however, are distorted and twisted beyond recognition. This idea, therefore, of the transference of the throne to the British Isles is pure fiction and has no legitimate support from the Bible or secular history.

In concluding this section, it should be pointed out that many of the verses used by British-Israelism and the Worldwide Church of God in constructing their theory have been adequately refuted in such books as *The Delusion of British-Israelism* by Anton Darms, and the classic by David Baron, *The History of the Ten "Lost" Tribes*. It has been impossible in this presentation to mention and refute the many misused and misapplied verses. However, it should also be noted that the key verses used by the old British-Israelite theorists in building their system are identical to the ones found in Herbert Armstrong's *The United States and British Commonwealth in Prophecy*. Therefore, though these works mentioned above are not directed toward the Worldwide Church of God, they still adequately answer it.

The Persons of the Godhead in Armstrongism

God the Father in the Old Testament

It is the position of Armstrongism that there are now just two persons in the Godhead, the Father and the Son. In the Old Testament, Jesus Christ was Jehovah, and it is Christ who always spoke and was seen of men. This is true, according to Armstrongism, because no man has seen or heard the Father, and because Christ is the Word, the "spokesman" of the Godhead. This teaching is based primarily on John 1:18 and 5: 37. It is stated that the Father, even before the incarnation, was in supreme command of the Godhead, but played no real role in the affairs of men[33]

This view of God confuses the persons in the Godhead and relegates the Father to a role of practical unimportance especially in relationship to men in the Old Testament. Armstrongism puts such an emphasis on the distinct persons involved that no real unity is seen in the Godhead, almost to the point that there are two Gods.

The claim is made that it was Jesus Christ who always spoke and was seen of men in the Old Testament. First, it ought to be recognized that John 1:18 does not teach the inactivity of the Father. It simply states that no human being has actually, visibly seen the Father. John 5:37 is used to show that no man has heard the Father's voice, therefore, proving that any divine communication with man was done by Jesus Christ. This verse, however, has nothing to do with the audible voice of the Father. The context clearly is speaking of the Father's voice, or witness, through the Scriptures.

The Jews of Jesus' day had not "heard" it. In point of fact, the Father's voice had been heard not too long before this at the baptism of Christ.

It is true, of course, that Christ is seen as one with Jehovah. Yet he is also distinct from Jehovah. In several places in the Old Testament, it is recorded that Jehovah spoke to Jehovah or with the "angel of Jehovah" (e.g., Zech. 2:8, 9). Armstrongism agrees that the Angel of Jehovah is deity, and is in fact Christ (Ex. 3; Gen. 16, and 22 reveal the Angel of Jehovah to be deity), but since the Angel of Jehovah does appear to men, then the Father must be Jehovah in those Scriptures where two divine persons are involved. It is interesting to note that the Holy Spirit is also equated with Jehovah (Jer. 31:31-34 with Heb. 10:15). Both the Father and the Son can be designated Jehovah, though distinct persons, because of the divine attribute of unity. The point here is not to argue that Christ of the New Testament is never equated with Jehovah of the Old Testament, because He obviously is in a number of places, notably in Hebrews. The point is that God the Father was active in the affairs of men generally and Israel in particular. Armstrongism arrived at this position by taking a very few verses and neglecting to balance them with the total scope of the Scriptures.

In defining Christ as the "spokesman" for the Godhead, Armstrongism is in error. As a lexicon will reveal, Christ is the "Word" in the sense that He is the full, complete and perfect expression of the unseen God. He is the personal manifestation of Deity, not the one who does the talking for the Godhead.

It must be concluded that the view of the Worldwide Church of God is confused and in error. Verses that are used as proof texts are used in a superficial way with little regard for the context. Words are defined with little regard for established meanings. This confusion concerning the Godhead sends waves of error into the other areas of doctrine.

The Name "Elohim"

One of the basic tenets of Armstrongism in its doctrine of God is that the plural noun *Elohim* is to be understood as a "God-Family"; a family which true Christians will eventually join.

> *Elohim* is a uniplural or collective noun, such as "church," or "family," or "kingdom." In other words, *Elohim* stands for a SINGLE CLASS composed of TWO or MORE individuals. *Elohim*, then, is the "God Kingdom" or "God Family."[34]

It is reasoned that since the plural of the word is used it must mean that more than one person is in view. Then it is assumed that the plural puts it into the category with such words as family or kingdom, which obviously have more than one individual in them. The next step is then to demonstrate that Christians will eventually become members in the "God Family" equal in every way to Jesus Christ.

The name *Elohim* is indeed plural, but it is not nearly as elastic as Armstrongism would wish. This word is the general Hebrew name for God and is used over twenty-five hundred times in the Old Testament. Although it is also used of men and idols, it is employed in over twenty-three hundred of these instances of the true God. Although it is plural, and thus opens the way to the concept of the Trinity, it is usually used with a singular verb, stressing the oneness and unity of God.[35] It would, therefore, seem legitimate to say that the biblical emphasis of oneness is different from Armstrongism's emphasis on plurality. The idea of persons within the Godhead is obviously there, but awaits the New Testament for expansion, explanation and definition. As the theologian, A. H. Strong, comments,

> And God's purpose in securing this pluralization may have been more far-reaching and intelligent than man's. The Holy Spirit who presided over the development of revelation may well have directed the use of the plural in general, and even the adoption of the plural name Elohim in particular, with a view to the future unfolding of the truth with regard to the Trinity.[36]

The Hebrew lexicons of Gesenius, and of Brown, Driver and Briggs make it clear that a "God Family" is not inherent in this word. Again it can be observed that Armstrongism has not been true to the biblical definition of a word, but has instead ignored established meaning and stretched the word far beyond its limits.

The Worldwide Church of God is also in error in seeing just two persons in the Godhead now. The Old Testament hints at it and the New Testament reveals it: there are three persons in the Godhead now and forever. The deity of the Holy Spirit will be discussed in the next section.

The final step in the theory of the Godhead in the theology of the Worldwide Church of God is that men will actually become God. This, however, is impossible unless the definition and concept of God is completely altered from the God of the Bible. God has certain properties intrinsic to Himself by which He is identified or distinguished. These attributes are the elements that characterize God and make it possible to identify Him as God. There is simply no way that man can possess these attributes. One is left with one of two alternatives: either man cannot become God or God must somehow be changed. Armstrongism, claiming loyalty to the Scriptures, cannot tamper too much with the attributes of God. It is then left with the dilemma (which it doesn't seem to recognize) of getting man to obtain the attributes of God. This supposedly transpires at the resurrection when believers become "like Christ." However, it is obvious that there are certain facts that not even the resurrection can change. The view of the Worldwide Church of God is that men become spirit beings at this time, and thus they become God-like. However, even becoming a spirit creature (which is not what occurs at the resurrection) does not endow men with the attributes of God. If there is but one attribute of God that man cannot obtain, then he is less than God and not God. A brief glance at several intrinsic properties of deity will quickly reveal that man can never be the possessor of them.

Man depends on God for life and therefore does not have the attribute of *self-existence,* which is a characteristic of God.

> God is self-existent, that is, He has the ground of His existence in Himself . . . As the self-existent God, He is not only independent in Himself, but also causes everything to depend on Him. This self-existence of God finds expression in the name Jehovah. It is only as the self-existent and independent One that God can give the assurance that He will remain eternally the same in relation to His people.[37]

Man owes his existence to God and is not independent in himself. The resurrection does not change the fact that man is a creature.

God does not change, but all men do, including the change that takes place at the resurrection. God is immutable.

> By this we mean that the nature, attributes, and will of God are exempt from all change. Reason teaches us that no change is possible in God, whether of increase or decrease, progress or deterioration, contraction or development. All change must be to better or to worse. But God is absolute perfection, and no change to better is possible. Change to worse would be equally inconsistent with perfection. No cause for such change exists, either outside of God or in God Himself.[38]

God is characterized by eternity. He is the eternal God and is from everlasting to everlasting. Man, on the other hand, had a beginning, even though he will not have an ending. The resurrection cannot change the fact that a man has not always existed. It cannot give to man the attribute of eternity. Men cannot, therefore, become God.

Other attributes of God could be presented, but the point has been made. Man cannot, by any stretch of the imagination or the Scriptures, become God. Armstrongism has deviated seriously from the truth in its concept of God and man. Along with Mormonism, it attempts to raise man to the level of deity, but in the process must lower God to do it. Both theology and linguistics are against Armstrongism in its concept of the "God Family."

The Deity of the Holy Spirit

In summarizing the doctrines of the Worldwide Church of God it was noted that there was a denial of the deity and personality of the Holy Spirit. The Spirit was viewed as a force, as the power and mind of God.[39] Armstrongism defends its position by pointing out that "spirit" is neuter and not masculine and concludes that this indicates that the Spirit is not a person. This is true, it is stated, even in passages where "he" is used. This is explained by an Armstrongite writer.

> In the above passages (John 14:16; 16:17, 13) the Holy Spirit is referred to as the "Comforter." "Comforter" is masculine in the Greek—just like the many other *in*animate objects, like stone, which are also masculine. According to Greek rules of grammar you must use a masculine pronoun to refer to a masculine noun. Since "comforter" is masculine in Greek, a masculine pronoun is used.[40]

In answering the position of Armstrongism on the use of the neuter very little needs to. be said. It is obvious that the neuter word *spirit* should be substituted by a neuter pronoun. This is the normal pattern of Greek grammar and one would expect that this would always be the case. However, contrary to grammatical rules, the masculine pronoun is used in several Scriptures, making the Spirit's personality the clear intent of the writer. The masculine demonstrative pronoun is used in John 16:13 and 14; "howbeit when he" or "howbeit when that person" (verse 13), and "he shall glorify me" or that "person shall glorify me" (verse 14). In John 15:26 and Ephesians 1:14 the masculine relative pronoun is used for the neuter "spirit." This use of the masculine is evidence to justify the conclusion that He is a person.

The position on the Holy Spirit that is held by the Worldwide Church of God is not new. The error is the ancient one of the Socinians. The Socinians denied the personality and deity of the Holy Spirit, but regarded the Spirit as the influence of the eternal God. Since this is an ancient doctrinal error, much has been written in answer to it. In order to prove that the Holy Spirit is God, two biblical facts must be demonstrated. First, it must be shown that the Holy Spirit is a person, thus demonstrating that He is not merely a force or power. Second, it is necessary to prove the Spirit's deity, thus showing that He is a person who is on an equal plane with the Father and the Son.

The Bible reveals that the Holy Spirit is a person by attributing actions to him that cannot be the expression of a power or a thing. The Holy Spirit participated in creation (Gen. 1:2); He teaches and brings truth to remembrance (John 14:25); He guides (Rom. 8:14); He prays (Rom. 8:26); He guides into all truth, and hears, speaks, and shows (John 16:13); He spoke to Philip (Acts 8:28); He gives authoritative commands (Acts 13:2, 4). The Scriptures also view the Spirit as a person by recording that He possesses the essential attributes of personality. The Holy Spirit has intelligence (I Cor. 2:10, 11); emotions (Eph. 4:30); and will (I Cor. 12:11). Further, the Spirit is a person because He can be treated like one. The Spirit can be sinned against (Isa. 63:10); He can be reverenced (Ps. 51:11); He can be lied to (Acts 5:3); He can be resisted (Acts 7:51); and He can be obeyed (Acts 10:19-21).

The verses in this section are but a few of the many that could be set forth to give proof of the Spirit's personality. The feeble grammatical arguments of Armstrongism do not prove its case.

Once the personality of the Holy Spirit is demonstrated, the next step is to show that He is God. Several lines of argument are usually followed. The Holy Spirit is identified with the title of Jehovah (Isa. 6:8, 9 with Acts 28:25; Jer. 31:31-34 with Heb. 10:15); He is called God (Acts 5:1-4); the Christian indwelt by the Spirit is indwelt by God (I Cor. 3:16; 6:19; Eph. 2:22); He is placed on an equal plane with the Father and Son ("name" is singular in Matt. 28:19); He possesses the attributes of deity, such as omniscience (I Cor.

2:10, 11), omnipresence (Ps. 139:7), and omnipotence (Zech. 4:6); He does work that only God can do, such as creating (Gen. 1:2), regenerating (John 3:6), and sanctifying (II Thess. 2:13). The Holy Spirit, then, is God, according to the Scriptures.

The doctrine of the Godhead in the theology of the Worldwide Church of God is confused and unbiblical. It should be evident from this brief discussion that Armstrongism does not allow the Scriptures to speak for themselves in the normal meaning of the words, and in sound exegesis built on established grammatical principles. These doctrinal deviations have affected the other divisions of theological truth.

The Nature and Destiny of Man in Armstrongism

In its view of man the Worldwide Church of God adopts the view of conditionalism, along with the Seventh-day Adventists and Jehovah's Witnesses. Conditionalism teaches that man was created as a living soul with the potential for immortality. It believes that man *is* a soul but does not allow the soul to be considered as a separate entity. Conditionalism further teaches that sin brought death to man, but immortality can be gained by accepting God's provision and fulfilling His will. The penalty of sin is death, which is cessation of being, or "sleep." Conditionalism states that the righteous will be resurrected to immortality and life, while those who refuse God's ways will receive eternal punishment, which is annihilation. These are the basic principles of conditionalism which are held by the Worldwide Church of God.

The Nature of Man
The Concept of Immortality

The Worldwide Church of God believes that man only receives immortality when he responds to the conditions established by God. These terms of salvation will be discussed in the section on "Salvation and the Law."

Several points are made regarding immortality. First, it is

the observation of Armstrongism that not once is immortality spoken of in connection with a soul or spirit. "Having proved the usage of *both* the Hebrew and Greek words, we can see there is not one single place in the entire Bible where soul has anything to do with immortality."[41] This seems to be a vital point as it is often mentioned in one way or another. Second, it is often pointed out that if man has a soul that is immortal, why then is immortality spoken of as future and why is man encouraged to seek it?

> The word "immortality" is used only in five places in the Bible: Romans 2:7; 1 Cor. 15:53, 54; 1 Tim. 6:16 and 2 Tim. 1:10. STUDY those Scriptures. In each case, immortality is something that is *brought to light*, that must be *obtained*, that God ONLY has, and in no case is something man already possesses![42]

At first these points seem unanswerable, but in reality they carry no weight at all. It must always be remembered that scripturally the attribute of immortality is applied only to the body, and orthodoxy agrees that this bestowing is still future. In this respect, it is not the present possession of man and it does await the day of resurrection. Although the term immortality itself is applied to the material body in the Scriptures, this does not remove the idea of the immaterial part of man existing separately after the death of the body.

> What Scripture does support is that man, once created, does possess a quality (soul or spirit) which can exist as a conscious entity apart from the body and which will continue in its existence through all eternity.[43]

Although the term "immortality" is not applied to man, the underlying truth is still there, just as the word "Trinity" is nowhere used to describe God, yet is nevertheless a true concept.

> And what is more important, while the Scriptures do not apply to man the word "immortal," they do apply to him the word *life* which has a deeper and richer concept.[44]
>
> What is the relationship between this human mortality and what is called the "immortality of the soul"? It is clear that the affirmation of this immortality is not meant to deny man's dying,

but rather speaks at the same time of man's death and of the immortality of the soul. That is the unique and complicated situation in which this expression places us, and which constantly gives rise to the question whether we can actually speak of the mortality of man, and whether perhaps we would not do better to speak of the mortality of a part of man.[45]

While the "immortality of the soul" is not a phrase to be found in the Bible, this does not rule it out as a biblical concept, nor does it or should it remove it from the language of theology. Orthodoxy recognizes that this is a complicated issue, but refuses Armstrongism's contention that since the word "immortality" is never used of the soul, then the soul is therefore not immortal.

Another argument of the Worldwide Church of God regarding immortality rests on I Timothy 6:15, 16 where it is recorded that, ". . . the King of kings, and Lord of lords; who only hath immortality, . . ." This is a key text that is used to prove that only God, and not man, has innate immortality as an attribute. "Your Bible tells you that ONLY God has immortality."[46] However, this passage does lose its force for the Armstrong position when it is remembered that God's attributes can never become man's to the same degree or quality. Man's immortality is obviously not the same as God's.

> None of the divine perfections are communicable in the infinite perfection in which they exist in God, . . . none of the attributes of God are incommunicable in the sense that there is no trace of them in man, and that none of them are communicable in the sense that they are found in man as they are found in God. . . .[47]
> . . . we acknowledge that in the strictest and highest sense God alone has immortality, in that He alone has existed from eternity and will always exist. He is the only absolute Being. But when human souls were created in His image, while they have a beginning, they have no ending and are from that time on immortal. To be immortal means to be never-dying. Man's body is mortal; but his soul is immortal.[48]

In the Timothy passage the word means underived and eternal existence. This, obviously, could never be the possession of any man, since he is but a creature.

> The Bible says that God only hath immortality ... and this would seem to exclude the idea of human immortality. But it is perfectly evident from Scripture that man is also immortal in some sense of the word. The meaning is that God alone hath immortality as an essential quality, has it in and of Himself, while man's immortality is an endowment, is derived from God.[49]

One key proof text of Armstrongism is therefore, valueless in proving its point, since two different aspects are being discussed—the Timothy passage speaking of something which man never will possess.

Another factor having a bearing on the discussion of immortality is the concept and definition of eternal life. Armstrongism recognizes that eternal life has an important relationship to immortality and one's view of it. In its literature, Armstrongism equates the two.[50] Yet it is also the present possession of believers in the sense that as long as the Spirit remains with them they also have its "presence."[51] The implication is clear: that one who possesses eternal life also possesses immortality. This position is a natural one for Armstrongism to hold in light of its view that man does not have entities which can exist apart from the body. However, Walter Martin's comment on this position is helpful at this point.

> A study of these words in any Greek lexicon, and of their use in the New Testament, will show that immortality and eternal life are neither identical nor synonymous ... to treat these terms as interchangeable is clearly a linguistic impossibility.[52]

Eternal life is said to be the present possession of the Christian here and now. Armstrongism fails in its understanding of this truth. It attempts to relegate it to the future by saying that Christians are simply the heirs and not the possessors of eternal life. However, this is simply not the plain teaching of the Scriptures. It is difficult to understand how a person in any sense could be the possessor of eternal life and still possess it when he ceases to exist as a person. To put everything in the future is neither biblical, nor is it logical or reasonable in the light of the meaning of "eternal" life. Jesus said, "And this is life eternal, that they should know thee the only true God, and him whom thou didst send, even Jesus Christ" (John 17:3).

> *Life,* so defined, possesses various elements. It implies conscious-ness; for there is no knowledge without conscious existence. Fur-ther, it signifies *contact,* for one cannot apprehend those things with which one has neither direct nor indirect contact. Again, it involves *continuity* or duration, because knowledge of God pre-supposes coexistence with Him. And finally, it assumes *develop-ment* since the knowledge of God must be a growing, not a static thing. Eternal life, man's full destiny, is the object of the teaching of this Gospel.[53]
>
> For the believer, eternal life is a present possession, not a reward bestowed at the gates of death.[54]

Orthodoxy acknowledges with the Apostle Paul that our salvation is not yet complete, as long as we remain in our mortal bodies (Rom. 8:18-25). We await immortality in this sense. However, the Scriptures are equally clear that we, as believers, now possess eternal life (e.g., John 3:16, 36; 5:24; 6:40, 47, 54; I John 5:11-13). Eternal life and immortality, in biblical usage, are not equivalent terms the one applying to man's immaterial part and the other to the material.

Armstrongism, of course, rejects the idea that such a dis-tinction can be made between the material and the imma-terial parts of men. It rejects the concept as "pagan dualism." It seeks to prove its case on the basis of word studies, pri-marily those found in the Old Testament.

The Concept of "Soul"

Armstrongism's view of man is strictly a materialistic one. In discussing the soul (נֶפֶשׁ), it points out with undisguised enthusiasm that this term is used of brute animals as well as of man.

> The original Hebrew word for "soul" is nephesh. Bagster's *Analyt-ical Hebrew and Chaldee Lexicon* defines it as "breath," and "anything that breathes, *an animal,*" ... In Genesis 1:21, 24; 2: 19; 9:10, 12, 15, 16, and Leviticus 11:46, the same word *nephesh* is translated "creature" when referring to *animals.* And so man is a creature; man *is* a SOUL. Animals are creatures or souls,

> too! . . . The "soul," then is merely animal life that is subject to death and decay.[55]

The point simply being that if "soul" signifies immortality, then animals too possess immortality. Armstrongism discusses this word a great deal. When coming to the New Testament, the interpretation of this Old Testament word dictates the meaning of the New Testament word for soul ($\psi\nu\chi\acute{\eta}$).

> Soul in the Greek, comes from psuche, which means "breath." The word comes from the root *psucho* which is the Greek verb, "to breathe." Thus, it corresponds exactly to the Hebrew *nephesh* which means the temporary life of animals.[56]

Armstrongism, then, does not believe that the soul is something which is separate from the body, nor as a result does it hold to its immortality. It believes that "soul" is a reference to the whole man.

It is the conclusion of this writer that Armstrongism commits a very basic error in its study of "soul"; that of forcing a word into a restricted meaning and then building upon this narrow meaning a superstructure of doctrine. The problem for orthodoxy comes when the Worldwide Church of God is not challenged on its word studies. Once allowed this foundation, the superstructure is far more difficult to topple.

Another observation is that Armstrongism will usually interpret the Old Testament in light of the New. However, this is clearly not the method when the issue of conditional immortality is discussed. It insists on dictating the meaning of New Testament words by its rigid definitions derived from Old Testament texts that lack the clarity of progressive revelation. The New Testament is far clearer and definitely more developed on the subject of life after death, and ought to be used in interpreting the Old Testament portions that are less clear.

The Armstrongite view is not the biblical one. The Bible views "soul" in a variety of ways. While it can simply mean "life" it is also used to refer to that immortal part of man that exists apart from the body, even when the material body dies.

First, it is quite evident that immaterial does not need material in order to function. This is a basic observation that must be made.

> The Bible teaches that there is an intelligent spirit in man, which exists in a conscious state after the death of the body. What is a spirit? Jesus said, "God is a spirit." . . . Here, then, is one intelligent, conscious, immortal spirit which has neither flesh nor bones . . . Our spirits . . . are from a different source, and of a higher nature than our bodies.
>
> So the Holy Spirit, the third person in the Trinity, is an intelligent, immortal spirit, without flesh and bones.
>
> The angels are conscious, intelligent persons, yet they are spirits. "Who maketh his angels spirits." Heb. 1:7. So the devils are spirits; yet they are intelligent persons and do not die. See Mark 5:1-13. . . . This shows that spirits are intelligent persons. not merely air, or breath, or an influence. . . .[57]

Therefore, that which is immaterial can and does exist apart from that which is material, but does this truth extend to man? There are numerous texts that show this true of man; that his soul does have separate existence when the body dies. Several passages will illustrate this.

(1) Genesis 35:18—"as her soul was departing (for she died)." This supports the orthodox view on both points: that the soul can exist apart from the body, and that death does not mean cessation of being.

(2) I Kings 17:22—"the soul of the child came into him again." Norman Douty, refuting Seventh-day Adventism, comments on this passage and the one from Genesis 35.

> . . . Adventists insist that God never put soul *into* man, that He only made man *to be* soul, but by putting breath of spirit into him. Thus, refusal to admit that the word "soul" is sometimes used in the sense of personality involves them in difficulty. The statements of the Scriptures are explicit: Rachel's soul went out of her and the boy's soul came into him again. Both indicate existence apart from the body.[58]

(3) Matthew 10:28—"Be not afraid of them which kill the body, but are not able to kill the soul."

> In this passage *psuchee* cannot be another name for the whole person . . . for, if so, the *psuchee* would be dead when the body is

killed. What Jesus is saying here is this: There is something about you which those who kill you cannot touch! That something is that aspect of man which continues to exist after the body has been lowered into the grave![59]

(4) Revelation 6:9-11—"And when he had opened the fifth seal, I saw under the altar, the souls of them that were slain for the word of God. . . . And they cried with a loud voice, saying, How long, O Lord, holy and true, dost thou not judge and avenge our blood on them that dwell on the earth? And white robes were given unto everyone of them; and it was said unto them that they should rest yet for a little season, until their fellow servants also and their brethren, that should be killed as they were, should be fulfilled." This passage records the prayer of those who had suffered martyrdom because of their unwavering witness for God. The context would indicate that these died during the early days of the Tribulation period. Clearly they died before the breaking of the fifth seal. This scene takes place before their resurrection, which therefore pointedly teaches that they are existing after physical death. They have died, but their bodies have not yet been resurrected, yet they are very much alive. In this text "soul" refers to souls of individuals.

> If *psuchas* here was intended to stand for persons, we would expect that the case of the perfect passive participle which follows would be the same as that of the word *psuchas*, so that the passage would read, "the slain persons," or "the persons that had been slain." Instead, the participle is in the genitive case (esphagmenoon), so that the words must be translated, "the souls *of* them that had been slain." The reference here is obviously to the *souls of people* who have been slain as martyrs for their loyalty to God—to souls, in other words, who still exist after death and who are conscious.[60]

The resurrection hasn't come because their persecutors are still living and because they are informed by God that there is yet some time to be completed in His program. Neither the Second Coming, nor the resurrection which accompanies that coming has taken place yet.

The Worldwide Church of God teaches that the fifth seal

begins the Great Tribulation and is prior to the Second Coming and the "first resurrection." It is faced with a problem of having martyrs who are alive before the resurrection. This passage is conveniently explained away as an allegory.[61]

Other passages could be added to these given here.[62] Other major portions will be dealt with later when the soul's experiences at death is dealt with. The point here is simply that man *possesses* a soul as well as being a soul. Closely related to a discussion of the soul is that of the spirit.

The Concept of "Spirit"

Armstrongism believes that the "spirit" in man is the same as the "breath of life." The body lives when the breath, or spirit, enters and it dies when the spirit or the breath departs.

> Notice that in this verse the Bible refers to "spirit" as common to both man and beast (Eccl. 3:20). This word "spirit" comes from the Hebrew word *ruach* and is translated 28 times as "breath." . . . The same Hebrew word is translated 90 times as "wind." It is simply the "breath" which is common to both men and animals. When they die, they both "expire"—their breath leaves them.[63]

It is argued that those who possess the breath of life, or spirit, are subject to death.

> While a man is still alive, the Bible speaks of his breath as being in the hand of God . . . (Job 12:10). And so, when a man dies, he figuratively gives up his *breath* to God.[64]

It is interesting to note what is not said in the literature of the Worldwide Church of God on this subject of the spirit. There is no meaningful discussion of the New Testament word πνεῦμα. Yet, πνεῦμα with its great variety of meanings sheds much light on the discussion, contributing significantly to an understanding of the immaterial part of man.

The spirit of man is seen as a separate entity in numerous places in the New Testament. Some examples are given.

(1) Luke 8:55—"And her spirit came again, and she rose straightway."

(2) I Thessalonians 5:23—". . . your whole spirit and soul and body be preserved blameless. . . ."

(3) Luke 23:46—"Father, into thy hands I commend my spirit."

> To commend one's breath to the Father is meaningless. To commend one's state of mind also makes little sense. By a process of elimination we discover that the only meaning of *pneuma* that makes sense here are soul, or spirit as part of the human personality. Jesus thus commends or entrusts his human soul or spirit to the Father.[65]

(4) Acts 7:59—"Lord Jesus, receive my spirit." Stephen's prayer at death is similar to Jesus' and only makes sense if spirit is part of the human personality.

(5) Hebrews 12:23—"the spirits of just men made perfect."

> . . . speaks of the redeemed who are not yet clothed with a resurrection body, but who are enjoying conscious fellowship with God in this state.[66]
>
> *Pneumasi*, the dative plural of *pneuma*, cannot here mean angels, since angels have just been mentioned. Neither can *pneumasi* designate people still on earth, for (1) why should the author describe people on earth as spirits? If he had intended to refer to people on earth, why did he not simply write *dikaiois teteleioomenois* ("to just men made perfect")? . . . The reference here is clearly to the spirits of just or righteous men, who are said to have been perfected, to have been brought to their goal (*telos*).[67]

Again, other references could be brought forward as evidence for an immaterial part of man which is a separate entity from the material (see footnote 61). Others will be dealt with in the discussion of man's destiny. It is clear once again that Armstrongism has restricted the meaning of a word in order to fit a concept into its theological structure.

The Concept of "the Image of God"

In its treatment of the nature of man, the Worldwide Church of God spends little time on the "image of God." It stresses the material constitution of man to such a degree that it finds itself in an uncomfortable position when dealing with man as created in God's image and likeness. The emphasis that man and animal are the same, both consisting of the dust of the ground and the breath of life, makes its statements on the superiority of man seem artificial and forced. Obviously if the material substance is the same and there is no immaterial substance which exists apart from the material, any attempted distinctions in the realm of the immaterial are nearly impossible since its framework does not allow for them.

Armstrongism distinguishes between the two words involved. The word "likeness" means that man was shaped in the outward form of God Himself. Man alone is the exact "clay replica of God Himself."[68] It is difficult to fully comprehend Armstrongism's view at this point, since its view of the nature of God is unclear. It was noted above (in chapter 3) that God is viewed as a spirit, yet has shape and form. Evidently, God is seen as a spirit in a similar way that angels are viewed as spirits—spirit beings that can take on definite form and are limited to one place at a time.[69] However, if this is the case then the attribute of omnipresence has been altered from the scriptural definition. Biblically, God is everywhere present in person, not simply in force or power. The latter resembles a kind of pantheism where God is in everything. For God to have form in the same way as angels presents a tremendous problem to the Worldwide Church of God in the realm of God's attributes. It is doubtful that the theologians of the Worldwide Church of God have wrestled at all with this contradiction. The point is, however, that "likeness" has some sort of visible characteristics, in the view of Armstrongism.

The word "image" refers to the mind and character of God, according to Armstrongism.[70] However, even here the material aspect is stressed. Man alone was created with a brain suited to develop the mind and character of God. It is in the brain that man differs from the animals.[71]

The main thing Armstrongism wants to point out is that

the image of God does not mean immortality. It contends that immortality is an attribute of God alone and if the "image of God" includes immortality, then why not another attribute such as omniscience? However, as it has been pointed out previously, man never does and never will have the attributes of God to the same degree that God possesses them.

Armstrongism recognizes the problem of making man too much like animals, but it does not really have an alternative. It states that man and beast are very different,[72] but logically it cannot hold that position and still hold its purely materialistic view of man. Its doctrine of anthropology doesn't allow for it.

The Genesis account reveals that man's creation differs significantly from the rest of creation, including the animal world. Man alone was created in the image and likeness of God, thus indicating that man is closely patterned after his Creator. Even though man sinned and death became his lot, he did not lose the image of God (e.g., Gen. 5:1, 3; 9:6; I Cor. 11:7; and James 3:9). These Scripture verses have little meaning if man is simply one who has life when the "breath" of life comes and ceases to exist when it goes.

The doctrine of "the image of God" is not simple. However, there are several observations that can be made. Since God is spirit (John 4), the image must primarily refer to man's spiritual and moral likeness. In what sensible way could man be made in God's image and likeness if it were not primarily in the realm of the immaterial?

> God is Spirit, and it is but natural to expect that this element of spirituality also finds expression in man as the image of God. . . . The soul is united with and adapted to a body, but can, if need be, likewise exist without the body. In view of this we can speak of man as a spiritual being, and as also in that respect the image of God. In this connection the question may be raised, whether the body of man also constitutes a part of that image. And it would seem that this question should be answered in the affirmative. . . . We need not look for the image in the material substance of the body; it is found rather in the body as a fit instrument for

the self-expression of the soul. Even the body is destined to become in the end a spiritual body, that is, a body which is completely spirit-controlled, a perfect instrument of the soul.[73]

This presents a sensible and scriptural picture of the relationship between the material and immaterial in the image of
God.

Although the fact that "image" and "likeness" strongly
indicate an immaterial aspect to man, this in itself is not
positive proof of immortality. It does, nevertheless, give evidence of an immaterial part of man—evidence which is developed later in the progressive revelation of Scripture.

In the discussion of immortality and the nature of man,
Armstrongism bases its argument on the Creation account in
Genesis and then proceeds to other portions of the Scriptures. While one ought to begin at the beginning, it is a mistake to assume that a full blown doctrine of anthropology is
revealed there. Whereas progressive revelation is acknowledged elsewhere, it is clearly not a vital part in its argumentation on the issue of man's nature. Armstrongism seems to
assume that everything basic was given in the Old Testament
and that the New Testament must then be interpreted in light
of it. This assumption, along with its restriction of the meaning of biblical words, is the basic cause of this erroneous
teaching.

The Destiny of Man

Armstrongism's concept of the destiny of man grows
directly out of its view of man's nature. If man is thought to
have no immaterial part that can exist separately from the
material, then the theories of "soul sleep," the cessation of
being at death, and the annihilation of the wicked come quite
naturally. Armstrongism could have no other position than
that of cessation of being and "soul sleep" in view of its
position on the nature of man, and it comes quite logically to
its view of annihilation because of its concept of conditional
immortality.

The Concept of Death

All men will die because of the sin of Adam. Since man is only a body-organism which possesses the breath of life, it is obvious that when the breath of life departs, only the body is left. Thus Armstrongism's conclusion that at death the individual is no longer a living soul and he ceases to exist. A vivid description of life and death is given.

> When you take a breath of air, it passes through to your trachea, into the lungs. . . . There oxygen is absorbed from the air and goes into the bloodstream. . . . Each of your 60 trillion cells uses oxygen to "burn" your food and to create the energy needed to power your organs and muscles, and to maintain body heat. The life of man clearly depends on the blood, and the blood needs the *breath of life* to keep the body active and alive.
>
> How clear that when a man ceases to breathe the breath of life, his heart stops beating and circulating his life's blood, and he dies.[74]

Therefore, when man dies, he ceases to exist as a person. "Death is the *absence* of life, the cessation of life—not the continuation of life under different circumstances."[75]

To Armstrongism, death is the opposite of life. Life means being, and therefore, death is nonbeing.

Armstrongism also believes in a second death which is the reward of the wicked. The first time they die in their sins and the second time they die for their sins. Those who reject the ways of God will receive the second death, which is defined as annihilation. This will be discussed later.

The materialistic view of man's nature is quite obvious in Armstrongism's discussion of death. This clearly is the faulty foundation on which its teachings are built. However, another erroneous idea should be mentioned before the discussion continues. Armstrongism once again assigns its own restricted meanings to the words "life" and "death." However, these are not accurate definitions as the following quotations reveal.

> "Life," in scriptural and theological language, means not primarily continuation of existence, but a rich spiritual experience in

association with God; and likewise "death," in Scriptural and theological language, means primarily not cessation of existence, nor separation of body and spirit, but separation from God.[76]

. . . death, in the Scriptural sense of the term . . . does not imply an actual cessation or even suspension of existence. . . . Take then the example of the seed-corn. . . . Our Savior says: "Except a corn of wheat fall into the ground *and die,* it abideth alone;" . . . Now in these passages the term death is used in its obvious and ordinary import; and yet it does not imply even a suspension of vitality, for through the whole process of *death* the living germ retains its vital power. . . . They (the Seventh-day Adventists) employ similar equivocations respecting the term *life.* The Holy Spirit employs the term often in the sense of simple *existence,* and also uses it to signify *well-being.* . . . In the latter of these senses it is employed in such passages as the following: . . . Deut. xxx, 15, 19 . . . Ps. xvi, 11 . . . Prov. x, 16; xi, 12; xix, 23 . . . Matt. vii, 14; xix, 17 . . . John v, 40. . . .[77]

It might be better then to say that life is well-being and death is, therefore, the loss of well-being rather than cessation of being.

The Concept of the Intermediate State

The Worldwide Church of God believes that man ceases to exist at death and there is no conscious existence until resurrection. Two main points must be dealt with: (1) the definition of "sheol" and "hades," and (2) the view known as "soul sleep."

There is much writing in all Conditionalist literature on the subject of Sheol and Hades. They universally contend that these are not places of torment or conscious existence. Their view is that these are simply to be understood as references to the grave.

The original Old Testament Hebrew word *sheol* and the New Testament Greek word *hades* means the same thing—simply the *grave*. These words have been translated "grave" in many places in the Bible. "Hell" is an old English word . . . for the word then meant merely a HOLE IN THE GROUND which was covered up—a dark silent place—a *grave.*[78]

The word *hades* is never used in the Bible to refer to *gehenna* fire, or the final hell fire! It always refers to the GRAVE! The

> Old Testament Hebrew word translated "hell" is *sheol*. It has the same meaning as *hades* and refers to a grave or pit or hole in the ground.[79]

In reply to this view of Armstrongism, several points need to be mentioned. First, it is true that mistranslations of "hell" have not helped bring clarity to the situation.

> The mistranslation of *sheol* and *hades* by the *King James* translators is the basis for much of the argumentation . . . is built on the mistranslation of these two words and a misunderstanding of orthodoxy. The best way to clear up this problem . . . is to accept the readings of the *American Standard Version* which leave the words untranslated.[80]

Second, it must be agreed that these terms are never equated with *eternal* hell punishment. These words primarily denote the place of the departed. After a good discussion of these terms, Boettner concludes:

> Briefly, we may say that in the Old Testament Sheol usually means the grave, but sometimes the place of punishment, while in the New Testament Hades and Hell usually mean the place of punishment but sometimes the grave.[81]

Boettner had included "hell" in his discussion along with "hades" which accounts for his emphasis on punishment in the New Testament. Other terms besides *hades* are used to speak of eternal punishment. This, however, does not mean that sheol and hades cannot and do not include the ideas of consciousness and present punishment. The point is that they are not the biblical words used for *eternal* punishment.

Third, Armstrongism is wrong in thinking that these words can only refer to the grave.

> Sheol clearly means the grave in many passages, but it just as clearly does not mean the grave in many passages, but a place of judgment, in others. For example, in Ps. 9:17: "The wicked shall be turned into *Sheol* and all the nations that forget God." (But the righteous as well as the wicked go to the grave.) Again, in Prov. 23:14: "Thou shalt beat (thy child) with the rod and shall deliver his soul from *Sheol*." (But no parent can, by discipline, keep his child from the grave.) Does "the lowest *Sheol*" (Deut. 32:22) mean "the lowest grave?" Of course not.[82]

There are a number of passages that reveal consciousness and punishing in the intermediate state and these will be looked at in the section on soul sleep.

The doctrine of soul sleep is an integral part of Armstrongism. It has been observed already that Armstrongism's concepts of sheol-hades and death rule out any possibility of conscious existence between death and resurrection. Therefore, it has used the metaphor of sleep to picture the state of nonbeing during this period. This concept of the intermediate state is, of course, based on verses that speak of death as "sleep."

In answering this position, it is first necessary to point out that Armstrongism makes the same kind of mistake here that they do with the concept of immortality. The term "sleep" is used in a figurative sense of the body.

> Everyone acknowledges, of course, that the *body* does sleep until the resurrection, that is, it becomes unconscious, insensible. The sleep spoken of is that of the body, not of the soul. Those who teach soul sleep have simply confused the sleep of the body with that of the soul. Soul sleep is not taught anywhere in the Bible. In every instance in which the word sleep is used in connection with the dead the context makes it clear that it applies only to the body.[83]

Its whole view of soul sleep rests squarely on its view of man's nature, in that there is a denial of separate existence at death for the immaterial. When man is viewed as having both a material and immaterial part to him, it is easily seen that these words apply to the body and not to man as a person.

Second, Armstrongism builds this doctrine upon a metaphor which is hermeneutically unsound. Death is pictured as sleep in the New Testament, but one does not develop a doctrine from a figure of speech.

Third, the fact that a figure of speech is being dealt with should cause care in interpretation. It is evident that we are here dealing with a word that is giving the appearance of the situation. The dead person appears to be asleep as the body lies there. He can no longer function. Outwardly he appears to be asleep, and this is the kind of language that is used.

Fourth, the Scriptures often cited to prove this theory are not allowed to speak for themselves. Some examples are given.

(1) I Kings 2:10—"David slept with his fathers, and was buried in the city of David." David's body, not his spirit was buried. Man's spirit is not buried, as it goes upward to God (Eccles. 3:21; 12:7; and Ps. 9:10).

(2) Ecclesiastes 9:5-10—"The dead know not anything." However, this statement is limited by the context to "anything that is done under the sun," verse 6.

(3) Acts 2:34—"David is not ascended into the heavens." The context clarifies the situation. This is being said of his body: "He is both dead and buried and his sepulchre is with us."

Other passages are definitely not clear and must therefore be interpreted by clearer verses.

Fifth, the New Testament teaches that believers are "in Christ." Believers have been chosen in Christ (Eph. 1:4); united with him (Eph. 2:4, 5); Christ is in them (Gal. 2:20); they are in him (John 14:20); they die in Christ (Rom. 14:8); they are raised with him (I Cor. 15:22); and they are destined for glory with him (I Thess. 4:17). Furthermore, nothing can separate believers from him (Rom. 8:35-39), and that specifically includes death. Romans 14:8 states that whether we live or die we are the Lord's. It is difficult to see how one can be "in Christ" and in Christ's hand if that person no longer exists.

Sixth, there are some powerful Scripture portions which destroy the concept of soul sleep if taken at their face value. The best arguments against the view of Armstrongism are the positive declarations of the Scripture.

(1) II Corinthians 5:6-8—In the plainest of terms, the Apostle Paul states that at the time he dies and leaves this sphere of existence, he enters at once into the presence of the

Lord, but Armstrongism attempts to weaken Paul's words by claiming that the text does not indicate *when* these things take place.

> Paul did *not* say WHERE he would go or WHEN he could be with Christ. There is not one word mentioning heaven here, nor is there one word saying that he would be with Christ immediately.
>
> He says that "we groan, *earnestly desiring* to be clothed upon with our house from heaven"—the spiritual body received at the resurrection through the power of the Spirit of God from heaven. Paul, while still alive, was waiting for Christ to come the second time that we might be *delivered from this vile body of flesh* with which we are born and which causes us to sin. . . . He was burdened and was *glad to end* the difficulties of life by death. To die is gain! There is *no knowledge* of passing time. *The next moment is the resurrection!*[84]

This passage, however, nowhere suggests an intermediate state of unconsciousness for the Apostle. Paul states that while he continues at home in the body, he is also continually away from home as regards the Lord (present tense). His fellowship is therefore incomplete (v. 7). However, a moment of time is coming (aorist) when this situation will be changed and he will be present with the Lord and absent from the body. Certainly a rather clear reference to death. This passage then teaches that at the moment of death the believer enters into a state of close ($\pi\rho\delta\varsigma$) fellowship with the Lord.

> . . . both the tenses of the infinitives in verse 8 and the parallelism between verse 8 and verse 6 indicate that being present with the Lord does occur the moment one dies.[85]

Charles Hodge has a good discussion on this passage in his commentary on II Corinthians. He, too, supports this interpretation and shows that Paul's presence with the Lord is not a reference to the resurrection.

> The apostle is speaking of the grounds of consolation in the immediate prospect of death. He says in effect that the dissolution of the body does not destroy the soul or deprive it of a home. His consolation was that if unclothed he would not be found naked. While at home in the body he was absent from the Lord, but as soon as he was absent from the body he would be present with the Lord. It is so obvious that the apostle is here speaking of what takes place at death. . . .[86]

It is also plain that in this verse it is absence from the body and presence with the Lord, not the being changed from corruptible to incorruptible without dying, that he earnestly longed for; and therefore this verse shows that the subject treated of in the context is the change which the believer experiences at death, and not that which those who are alive shall experience at Christ's second coming.[87]

(2) Philippians 1:21-23—In these verses Paul reveals the longing of his heart. He desires to be with Christ. He recognizes that the believers need his ministry in their lives, but states that of the two choices, he would prefer being with Christ.

What does the Worldwide Church of God say about this passage?

Now Paul's statement in Philippians is clear. He was willing to remain alive for the sake of the Philippians who needed him as a teacher and apostle, even though he desired personally to be delivered from troubles by death to AWAIT THE RESURRECTION and be with Christ, which would seem to him the *next moment of his consciousness.* [88]

Armstrongism doesn't interpret this passage at face value. Paul's emphasis is on the positive aspect of being with Christ and not on the negative aspect of leaving his troubles behind. What would Paul gain by lapsing into the realm of unconsciousness and nonexistence? With his zeal for the salvation of men and the building up of saints, he would prefer life to an unconscious existence after death. Discussing the grammar of Philippians 1:23, Walter Martin shows that Paul anticipated being immediately in the presence of Christ when he died.

The preposition *eis to* plus the infinitive shows "true purpose or end in view"—the strong desire which causes Paul's dilemma. Both infinitives (analusai and einai) have one construction, so are *one* thought, *one* grammatical expression; literally, "my desire is unto the, *to depart,* and unto the, *to be with* Christ." In simple English, Paul's one desire has a twofold object: departure and being *with* Christ! If departure did not mean his immediate being with Christ, another construction would have been employed. It therefore seems impossible that soul sleep was in the mind of the

Apostle, since he desired to depart *from* his body and to spiritually enjoy the presence of the Lord.[89]

The use of the two infinitives connected by the copulative καί, united by the one definite article, makes it clear that Paul is relating these two ideas together. In the Apostle's thinking, departure (death) meant that he was to be in Christ's presence. There is absolutely no allowance here for any period of nonexistence.

(3) Luke 16:19-31—The story of the rich man and Lazarus is a crucial passage in this controversy. The impact of these words of Christ is felt throughout the Conditionalists' camp. As a result much time is devoted to neutralizing this passage. The Worldwide Church of God has devoted an entire booklet to it. In its discussion, Paradise ("Abraham's bosom") is the land of Palestine. This conclusion is arrived at by noting that Abraham is mentioned in the story and all promises to Abraham are linked to the land. The angels who came for Lazarus are identified with those at the Second Coming of Christ who return with the Lord. Therefore, it is concluded that Jesus is teaching about the kingdom at the Second Coming and not about heaven or some intermediate state. The rich man, according to Armstrongism, opened his eyes and experienced great terror and anguish at the time of his resurrection at the end of the millennium, when he saw the lake of fire and realized his fate.[90]

Once again the answer of Armstrongism to the passage is that Jesus did not say *when* these things would happen. However, a plain reading of the passage does not indicate that well over a thousand years transpires in this account. It should be noted as well that the rich man desired that Lazarus return from the dead and tell his brothers to avoid this place that he was in. This tells us two basic things. First, the resurrection had not yet taken place, since the request is for Lazarus to be resurrected and return. Second, life is still going on as it always did, since the brothers of the rich man were going about life as usual—certainly not an accurate picture of post-millennial activity.

Armstrongism insists on making "Abraham's bosom" mean the literal Palestine, when it is clearly a figure of speech. Armstrongism, itself, uses "bosom" in John 1:18 in a figurative sense.[91]

Armstrongism deals with this passage in a most arbitrary way. The teaching of this passage is so definitely against soul sleep that supreme effort is made to neutralize it. There is no respect for the plain meaning of the words, nor is there consideration of the context. One wonders how God could communicate the truth of the intermediate state in any clearer manner.

Jesus is speaking of the very real theological issues of life and death. Jesus pointedly teaches that at death these two men were not reduced to the common level of nonbeing. The story would lose its point and be very misleading. Whether this is a parable or an actual event, it still teaches that there is life immediately after death; that life is lived in a conscious condition after death; that in this life the lost and saved are eternally separated; and that the lost carry with them some memories of their earthly experiences.

> The diversified conscious existence of the rich man and Lazarus pictured symbolically in this parable, therefore, must be a reflection of conditions during the intermediate state. As such, the parable confirms what we have learned from other New Testament passages, namely, that believers immediately after death go to be with Christ in order to enjoy a provisional happiness in His presence (provisional because their bodies have not yet been raised), whereas unbelievers at death go at once to a place of provisional punishment.[92]

(4) Luke 20:38—The Sadducees not only denied the resurrection, but according to Acts 23:8 they denied the existence of the soul after death. Jesus in his encounter with them corrected both errors. According to Jesus' words, Abraham, Isaac, and Jacob could not have been in the condition of nonbeing when God appeared to Moses at the burning bush and identified Himself as their God. The point being that He was then the God of these men who had died physi-

cally hundreds of years before. Jesus then concluded that He is the God of the living.

(5) Luke 23:43—The meaning of Jesus' word to the thief on the cross is changed completely by Armstrongism. The change is made by moving the location of the comma and thus changing the meaning.[93] Jesus' statement normally reads, "Verily I say unto thee, Today shalt thou be with me in paradise." It is changed to read, "Verily I say unto thee today, you shall be with me in paradise." By shifting the comma the words of the Lord are made redundant.

> Instead of a long unconscious sleep he had the assurance that that day he would be with Christ in Paradise. The spirit of Jesus went immediately to the Father, and with him went the spirit of this poor victim, saved by faith. To transpose the word "today" . . . making the verse read, "Today I say unto thee, thou shalt be with me in Paradise," is characterized by the best exegetical authorities as entirely unauthorized and as simply forcing the sense of the passage.[94]

If this is not the sense of this promise, then the words of Jesus would hardly have comforted him as he faced death. Obviously the thief knew the Lord was speaking to him "today" and the emphasis is meaningless. Also, Jesus used the word "verily" at the beginning of his statement to the thief, and he never qualifies that word because it would be unnecessary to do so.

(6) Luke 23:46—"Father, into thy hands I commend my spirit." This verse is meaningless if it applied only to the "breath" of Jesus.

(7) II Corinthians 12:2-4—Now whether Paul was in the spirit or not in his view of the "third heaven," we do not know since Paul, himself, did not know, but obviously Paul believed a man *could* be out of the body and go to heaven and hear such words.

Other passages could be brought in here in order to support the position that the immaterial consciously exists after death, but most of the main ones have at least been surveyed. Detail has been impossible, but good exegetical commentaries deal with the important words, tenses and constructions that bear out the position of the immortal soul.

The Concept of Annihilation

Unbelievers who reject the truth of God will suffer the fate of annihilation, according to the Worldwide Church of God. These will be involved in the "second death" which will cause them to cease their existence forever. By the time Armstrongism comes to this point on the destiny of the wicked it is assuming that its view of man's nature is correct.

It is held that "gehenna" is the "lake of fire" or second death. All sinners will be destroyed here. However, Armstrongism sets forth the idea that when the wicked are destroyed by fire, then the fires burn out.

> Since God said this fire "shall not be quenched" and since it is not burning today (referring to Jer. 17:27, the fire in Jerusalem's gates) it obviously went out *by itself* after accomplishing its purpose—after devouring all combustible material!
> They (the fires in the valley of Hinnom) were *never quenched* or put out by anyone! The flames merely died out when they had nothing more to consume. Even so, it will be with the FINAL *gehenna* fire. It will be unquenched—but it will finally burn itself out![95]

Any words, therefore, which speak of punishment or destruction of the wicked are interpreted to mean annihilation, but what of those terms when the word "eternal" or "everlasting" is attached to them?

> He (Jesus) used a Greek word—aionios—which comes from the Greek *aion,* meaning an "AGE." . . . The *aionios* fire Jesus spoke of refers to the age—ending fire which will occur at "the end of this world," and which will introduce the "world to come"! It is an *epochal* event! This is why Jesus calls it *aionios* or age-ending fire! The translation "everlasting" is misleading, since the fire itself will not burn forever.
> This terrible destruction . . . will consume and annihilate the wicked! . . . Nevertheless, the awesome EFFECT of this tremendous fire IS "eternal"—and is a witness for us, today! [96]

This reasoning is based entirely on the notion that immortality is conditional: "the wicked do not have immortality," therefore, "eternal punishment must look at the results and not the process." Perhaps this is oversimplifying the view of Armstrongism, but it nevertheless is a basically valid observation of its argumentation.

In response to this position some basic issues must be briefly discussed. First, logically, annihilation is not a punishment at all, but rather is something that would be desirable to the wicked. It is certainly not an adequate punishment for sin and the wicked would not feel constrained to cease sinning if their only punishment was a termination of consciousness. Second, Armstrongism's idea that the effects of the punishment are eternal is a meaningless distinction. If the sinner ceased to be, what would be the sense of the words "eternal" and "punishment"? If these words do not teach the eternal punishing of the wicked, it is difficult to see how this concept could be communicated in the Scriptures. Furthermore, the concept of annihilation does not come out of words such as "perish" or "destroy." These words mean to ruin or to render unfit for use.[97]

The main battleground is not over what seems logical, but rather over the use of biblical words. A survey of several key words will show that the wicked suffer eternal punishing and not annihilation with supposed eternal results.

The first important word is ἀπολλύμι. Armstrongism uses Matthew 10:28 ("destroy both body and soul in hell") to prove that ἀκολλύμι means annihilation—since the soul is destroyed too, but ἀπολλύμι has several meanings as Anthony Hoekema outlines so well; none of which can mean annihilation.[98] It can mean "lost" as in the case of the lost things in the Luke 15 parables. It can be applied to that which has become "useless," as in the case of the wineskins in Matthew 9:17. It also can be translated "kill" as in Matthew 2:13 where Herod sought to kill the babies in Bethlehem. Furthermore, when viewing Luke 9:24 which speaks of the saving or losing of life, annihilation cannot be in the passage or else the saved person is the one being annihilated. When we come then to passages which look at the future of the wicked and which use ἀπολλύμι, it should be translated the same as in other places and not have a new definition assigned to it. It would have to undergo a sudden change of meaning—a change clearly indicated in the context. However, this is definitely not the case and thus ἀπολλύμι does not support annihilationism.

A second key word is γέεννα, which refers to a place of fiery torment. Γέεννα pictures eternal punishment and is spoken of as an "everlasting fire" or "everlasting punishment" (e.g., Matt. 18:8; 25:41, 46; Mark 9:43). If the fire of γέεννα is eternal and if this symbolizes punishment, then the punishment is eternal as well.

This name was given to the valley south of Jerusalem. This Valley of Hinnom (as it is commonly referred to) came to be equated with the fiery judgment in apocalyptic literature. The human sacrifices to Moloch that were made there in the days of Ahaz and Manasseh (II Kings 16:3; 21:6; II Chron. 28:3; 33:6) and the coming judgments that would take place there (Jer. 7:32; 19:6) caused this valley to symbolize the place of eternal torment.[99]

It is necessary to distinguish Gehenna from Hades in order to fully understand its meaning.

> This distinction is . . . that Hades receives the ungodly for the intervening period between death and resurrection, whereas Gehenna is their place of punishment in the last judgment; the judgment of the former is thus provisional but the torment of the latter eternal (Mark 9:43 and par.: 9:48).[100]

While the description using this valley is figurative and symbolic, it is nevertheless a vehicle for conveying the meaning that the wicked will be punished in a place of torment forever.

A third word that enters into the discussion is κόλασις, which is properly rendered as "punishment." It is used in relationship to correction, torture and divine retribution but never of extinction.[101]

A fourth word is ὄλεθρος. This word carries the idea of ruin or destruction, but not of total extinction.[102]

> The noun rendered "destruction" . . . does not imply annihilation but carries with it the thought of utter and hopeless ruin, the loss of all that gives worth to existence. It does not denote loss of being but rather the loss of *well*-being, the ruination of the very purpose of their being. From 2 Thessalonians 1:9 it is clear that by destruction Paul does not mean physical annihilation but rather eternal separation from Christ of the lost. Destruction is the opposite of the salvation awaiting believers.[103]

A final word that must be mentioned is αἰώνιος. This word is usually rendered "eternal" or "everlasting." It is used of God in Romans 16:26; of divine possessions and gifts in II Corinthians 4:18; of the "eternal spirit" in Hebrews 9:14; and of the heavenly body in II Corinthians 5:1. These examples simply show that the word does have the idea of unending duration. It is an important word because it is frequently attached to words of punishment. Matthew 25:41, 46 gives a good example of usage. "Then shall he say also unto them on the left hand, Depart from me . . . into everlasting fire . . . (v. 41). "These shall go away into everlasting punishment, but the righteous into life eternal" (v. 46). Αἰώνιος is used in this one passage of both the righteous and the wicked. To be true to the text and grammar, either the existence of both is eternal or both face a limited duration. One cannot legitimately have the same word mean two entirely different things in this one context. If αἰώνιος applies to the never ending future of blessedness of the saints, it must follow that the wicked face future punishment that is equal in duration. Only clear grammatical evidence in the context could make it different, and no such evidence exists.

While this word study has been brief and not all words have been included, it nevertheless should demonstrate that the teachings of the Worldwide Church of God are not based on biblical words and concepts.

In concluding this section on the nature and destiny of man, it is clear that the mishandling of words through changing and restricting their meanings is the base on which this view of Armstrongism has been built. Its position on the destiny of man is the direct result of its view of the nature of man, and in neither case are they biblical views.

The Person of Christ in Armstrongism

Certainly one of the most vital areas of theology is that which deals with the person of Christ, as well as his work. Yet in this most crucial area the Worldwide Church of God holds positions that are contradictory to one another, besides being unbiblical and illogical. In an effort to deal succinctly with the errors of Armstrongism regarding the person of Jesus Christ, the problem will be studied in three areas.

The Deity of Christ

Unlike the Jehovah's Witnesses and other cults, the Worldwide Church of God clearly states that Jesus is God and that He is equal with God the Father, but then, based on John 14:28, it also states that the Father is greater. This statement, however, neglects to note that it was the Son of Man in His humiliation that spoke "the Father is greater than I." The Worldwide Church of God seems to believe that the Father always has been and always will be greater in authority, responsibility and office, with Jesus as second in command.[104] Since this is its stated position, then the Worldwide Church of God is dangerously close to polytheism. While the relationships between the persons of the Godhead transcend human comprehension, the Scriptures do not allow Christ to be viewed as "less" than the Father.[105]

The Incarnation and "Kenosis"

It was seen in the summary of Christology (chapter 3) that the Incarnation in Armstrongism differs from orthodoxy. In reality, Armstrongism does not have a God-man, but rather God was "converted" into a fleshly man. The distinction is so graphically made that there is no practical continuance of one person, but rather two separate persons. In orthodoxy, Jesus Christ became a perfect man while still being undiminished deity. In Armstrongism he was neither. He is seen as a human being with a fallen human nature, and as one who emptied himself completely of his deity. The Christ of Armstrongism, who lived on this earth, was a man possessing the fallen nature of man, but who, in some way, "exercised the character of God."

Armstrongism is incorrect in both areas of the person of Christ. Christ was a perfect human being. The New Testament clearly reveals that He experienced similar feelings, limitations, and needs as other human beings. He grew and developed normally, and nowhere in the New Testament does anyone doubt that He was a human being. Armstrongism blunders badly when it assumes that a man (even Jesus Christ) with a fallen nature is true man, when in reality he is less than the ideal man. The unfallen Adam was ideal and perfect humanity before sin damaged man and marred the image of God.

> Sinfulness is not a *necessary* characteristic of humanity, though it happens to be a universal characteristic of the humanity we know. Because this last is so, men are in the habit of regarding sinfulness and humanity as correlative terms.[106]

Christ was a perfect man who never sinned, nor could He sin. Possessing a fallen nature would have made Jesus Christ less than true man as God created him. Theologians have agreed that Christ never sinned, but have debated whether or not He could have done so. Those who believe He could have sinned (the position of Armstrongism) have assumed that temptability implies peccability. This is a correct assumption when dealing with man, even an unfallen one like Adam, but it is incorrect when dealing with the God-man. Christ was impeccable because He was that way by nature. The divine nature empowered the unfallen human nature, thus keeping the Person of Christ from sinning. This infinite power in the God-man assured Him continual victory.

> The idea that temptability implies susceptibility is unsound. While the temptation may be real, there may be infinite power to resist that temptation and if this power is infinite, the person is impeccable.[107]

It is not necessary to go into detail on this discussion, since this area of theology has been adequately dealt with in numerous works.[108]

The positive attribute of holiness in the God-man is found throughout the New Testament. Paul says that Christ "knew no sin" (II Cor. 5:21); John explains that the taint of sin was not to be found in His person (I John 3:5); Peter declared that He was righteous and did no sin (I Pet. 2:22; 3:18); the angel told Mary that He would be holy (Luke 1:35); Luke records that Christ is the Holy One of God (Acts 3:14; 4:27); Jesus, Himself, testified to His untainted character (John 8:29, 46; 14:30); and even demons testify to His holiness (Luke 4:34). Certainly these texts declare that the God-man in no way limited His attributes of holiness. He neither sinned nor adopted a sinful human nature.

Armstrongism also misunderstands the humanity of Christ because of its concept of man. It was seen in the previous section that in this view, man is a material being only. Christ, therefore, in His humanity had no immaterial aspects to Him. This clearly dictates the doctrine of the death of Christ in Armstrongism. This is why it makes the fallacious declaration that Jesus Christ, the Second Person of the Godhead, ceased to exist for three days and nights. Its erroneous doctrine of man causes it to take untenable positions in Christology.

Armstrongism is not only in error regarding Christ's humanity in the incarnation, but also His deity. It teaches that in the "self-emptying," or kenosis, Christ emptied Himself of being God. Christ temporarily gave up His attributes of deity. This position is impossible to hold and still retain the biblical doctrines regarding Christ and God. This position destroys the biblical concept of the Godhead, since one Person ceases for a time to be God. The Persons of the Godhead cannot be severed in this way without exchanging the biblical view of the Trinity for tri-theism. Armstrongism states that Christ divested Himself of inherent immortality.[109] Christ is therefore changeable, and therefore not God, since God is immutable. This position actually removes Christ altogether from being God. Christ without divine attributes is not God; this includes the times before and after the Incarnation. There are, of course, hundreds of other ramifications to this position which would destroy doctrine after doctrine like a row of falling dominoes.

The biblical doctrine of the Incarnation views Christ as perfect humanity united forever with undiminished deity. When Christ became a man, He "emptied Himself." This passage in Philippians does not give the details concerning of what the Son emptied Himself. He was in the "form of God" but took the "form of a servant." The word "form," $\mu o \rho \phi \acute{\eta}$, speaks of the external appearance or manifestation of a person or thing which accurately represents the underlying nature. Christ did not set aside this "form" of God, but rather veiled it by taking on the "form" of a servant and the "likeness" of man. This veiling limited the manifestations of deity, but in no way did it bring about any loss of deity. He did not lose His glory, but simply laid aside the external manifestation of it while retaining an inner glory. He did not lose His attributes but instead voluntarily did not exercise them independently. The English word "emptying" conveys the thought of pouring something out, but this Christ did not do. Nothing of His deity was poured out, even temporarily. To His deity was added humanity, and for a short season the full expression of His deity was hidden. Concerning His attributes, McClain says,

> It is better to say with Dr. Strong that Christ gave up the *independent use* of His divine attributes. This leaves room for all those exhibitions of divine power and knowledge which appear during His earthly ministry, and at the same time modifies in no essential respect the doctrine of a real kenosis.[110]

Therefore, it can be concluded that the position of the Worldwide Church of God is at total variance with the biblical view of the deity and humanity of the incarnate Christ.

The Resurrection of Christ

According to the Worldwide Church of God, Christ was raised a spirit being. Evidently, its reasoning is that only spirits can have immortality, and therefore Christ must have been raised as an invisible spirit. There also seems to be a touch of gnosticism in its writings, as they view the material body as essentially evil.

The word resurrection means a rising from the dead, presupposing that someone has died. Death affects the body alone and therefore the *body* must be involved if true resurrection is to take place. The nature of the body of the risen Christ is seen in two different ways in the Scriptures. First, the body of Christ manifested a spiritual aspect not true of it before. It was no longer limited by distance or space or such things as material barriers. Christ was able to appear and disappear at will. Yet, in spite of these things, the New Testament makes it clear that the resurrection body of Christ was the same one which was placed in the grave. Christ, after His resurrection, was recognized by His followers, except when for special reasons His identity was temporarily hidden. The resurrection body still contained the wounds in the hands, feet, and side. He ate food in front of His disciples, specifically pointing out that He was not a spirit (Luke 24:41-43). The body of Christ had a material nature so that it could be felt (Matt. 28:9; Luke 24:39). He breathed (John 20:22) and He stated that He had flesh and bones (Luke 24:39).

The Worldwide Church of God holds to a version of the old liberal error of the spiritual resurrection of Christ. This doctrinal deviation has been thoroughly exposed as an antiscriptural position. An accurate picture of the resurrection body has been given in a number of works.[111]

The New Birth in Armstrongism

The primary cornerstone in the soteriological structure of Armstrongism is its doctrine of the new birth. As a means of conveying its teaching, the comparison is made throughout its literature between physical and spiritual birth. A sharp distinction is created between begettal (conception) and actual birth. A person is begotten of God at the time of conversion, but will not be born until the resurrection. According to Armstrongism the new birth involves being changed into a spirit son of God, which gives to one immortality and divinity. The time between the conception and actual birth is this present life, which is seen as the gestation period. In the analogy, the Father begets sons and the Worldwide Church of God is the "mother" in whom the fetus develops. This development takes place as a result of obedience to the Ten Commandments, keeping the ordinances and growing in the teachings. Armstrongism uses a Greek word for birth as the basis of its teaching.

> Since the original Greek, in which the New Testament was written, has *only one word for both meanings*—and since the "scholars" of our comparitively recent years who translated the Bible into English did not, themselves, UNDERSTAND God's plan—they often translated the Greek word "gennao" into the English word "BORN" where it actually meant "BEGOTTEN."[112]

The statement is emphatically made that this is the only Greek word used to convey these meanings. Γεννάω is defined by Armstrongism.

> The Greek word is "gennao" ... The Greek-English dictionary ... gives this definition of the Greek word: *to procreate* ... *beget, be born, bring forth, conceive, be delivered of,* ...[113]

After emphasizing the difference between "beget" and "be born," γεννάω is then arbitrarily translated to fit into this theological mold translating it as "begotten" in every instance where believers are referred to in their human bodies. I John 3:9 is used as supporting evidence to prove that no one could now be born again. It emphasizes that the new birth has nothing to do with sin. New birth is simply the process which takes place at the resurrection whereby a mortal being becomes a spirit being. Jesus was a mortal man and He then became the spirit Son of God at the resurrection. To prove this, Romans 1:4 and 8:29 are employed. Romans 1:4 is made to say that Christ became the Son of God by the resurrection, and He is, therefore, "the firstborn among many brethren" (Rom. 8:29).

In answering this view of the new birth, it is essential to focus on Armstrongism's treatment of the Greek text. First, and quite important, is the fact that there are a number of words used in the New Testament which speak of birth besides γεννάω. Συλλαυβάνω is used of a woman's conception (Luke 1:24, 31, 36); τίκτω means to give birth or bring forth (John 16:21; Matt. 2:2; Rev. 12:4); ἀποκεύω from κύεω ("to be pregnant") and is used metaphorically of spiritual birth (Jas. 1:18); and ἀναγεννάω means born again, or from above (I Peter 1:3, 23). Other words and phrases are used in reference to conception (e.g., καταβολήν in Hebrews 11:11, and κοίτην ἔχουσα in Romans 9:10). Armstrongism is totally in error in its assertion that there is just one Greek word to express birth and conception.

Another point made by Armstrongism is that γεννάω can be used of a father's (or mother's) begettal. This, of course, is true, but armed with this fact, most appearances of this verb are then translated "beget." However, in checking a lexicon it is evident that the vast majority of times γεννάω is rendered "to be born." It is also interesting to find that the Lord used this verb in five places in the Gospel narrative, one of which is the pivotal passage of John 3. In the other four places, the context leaves no doubt that He is speaking of "birth." Why not then in the only other instance? Armstrongism is guilty of assigning meanings according to its theological bias. If there is only one word for both birth and begettal, as it erroneously contends, then it has no lexical basis for making distinctions. It cannot really argue or prove its point because

its position is based solely on its theology. Its theology assigns the meaning to γεννάω and then γεννάω is used to
prove its theology.

Peter's use of ἀναγεννάω is significant. In I Peter 1:3 and
23, ἀναγεννάω is found as a participle; once in the aorist (v.
3) and once as a perfect (v. 23). The perfect participle expresses a condition resulting from a completed action, while
the aorist can view the act as a simple or completed event. It
is not, according to Peter, the resurrection which brings
about new birth, but rather the Word of God, and, Peter tells
his readers, you have been born again already. He then en-
courages them to respond like the newborn ones they are
(ἀρτιγέννητα βρέφη) and desire the milk of the Word. Only
theological bias will keep one from seeing that here the new
birth happens in this life and not at the resurrection.

There is yet another fact that must be mentioned. The
concept of the new birth came out of an historical context
that must be considered. The semitic mind of New Testament
times would not have understood the new birth in the sense
of a gestation period. The idea of new birth was a concept
familiar to Judaism. When a non-Jew was converted to
Judaism, he was viewed as "a child just born." The proselyte
would then begin living as a new man, as one that had been
born again. For the first time he began to do the will of God
as a genuine man.[114] When, therefore, Jesus and the Apostles
spoke of new birth, their listeners would think of starting a
new life right then, not at some future day of resurrection.
The idea of a gestation period followed by a birth would be a
foreign concept to them. The idea of a birth followed by a
new life would be a concept more familiar to them. It must
be concluded that in manufacturing this teaching, Armstrongism has given little or no thought to the historic context of
this idea.

Much of the argument of the Worldwide Church of God
is actually built on the idea that Jesus became the Son of
God at the resurrection (Rom. 1:4). It is then concluded that

sonship must be received by man as well at the time of their resurrection.

The Bible does not teach that Jesus became a son at the resurrection. Jesus was the Son long before that time. In fact, Romans 1:3 says that He was born the Son—the Gospel is about "His [God's] Son, who was born." The Apostle held that Christ was the Son before the resurrection (Rom. 8:32; Gal. 4:4); the Messiah is called the Son (e.g., Ps. 2:7); Jesus acknowledged that He was the Son of God (Matt. 26:63); and the Father testified to this fact (John 1:34; Matt. 3:17). Romans 1:4 teaches that Christ was "proved to be" or "marked out as being" the Son of God. The mighty act of the resurrection "patently marked out" (Phillips) before men that Jesus Christ was indeed the Son of God. The resurrection accomplished many things, but it did not give him sonship—that He already possessed.

Concerning the passage used by Armstrongism in Romans 8:28, 29, very little needs to be said. Christ is the "firstborn among many brethren" not in the sense of coming first and being one among equals. Πρωτότοκος ("firstborn") expresses His preeminence and priority. In this passage His priority is seen in relationship to the Church.

Underlying much of the confusion in the soteriology of the Armstrong cult is its view of the nature and destiny of man. With man having no immaterial part that exists apart from material, salvation, of necessity, must be in the future tense exclusively. Man, who ceases to exist at death, cannot really possess salvation now, but must wait until he is "re-created" at a resurrection. Salvation, then, is very definitely a future thing in Armstrongism.

The Bible, however, presents salvation as a present possession of believers. Certainly salvation has a future tense (e.g., Rom. 8:23), but nevertheless it is also true that we "have been saved" by the grace of God (Eph. 2:8, 9). Many passages speak of salvation as a past or present possession of Christians (e.g., II Cor. 6:2; Rom. 1:16; 8:1; John 3:36; 5:

24; 6:47; 10:28; I Pet. 1:3, 18, 23; I Cor. 1:18; II Tim. 1:9). No one who is a Conditionalist can logically fit these two aspects of salvation into his soteriological system.

The conclusion must be that Armstrongism's concept of the new birth has no valid biblical base. The historical context, words and expressions, word usage, and verb tenses are all aligned against Armstrongism. Although its doctrine of salvation is found in error on this important issue, it is still necessary to look briefly at other aspects of its soteriology, particularly its view of the law. It will be seen that the Worldwide Church of God essentially teaches a salvation which is dependent upon works.

The Law in Armstrongism

The Law in Armstrongism's Salvation

The Mosaic law plays a significant role in Armstrongism's view of the plan of salvation. In chapter 3, that basic plan was given. It was seen to include a number of elements, but the Ten Commandments emerged as the pivotal factor in the soteriological system. To briefly review: the individual is "called" by God the Father and he responds in faith and repents of his sinful way of life, asking for forgiveness. When he does so, the death of Christ causes all his past sins to be removed. He actually becomes converted or "begotten" when he receives the Spirit of God at the time of water baptism. The individual is not able to understand spiritual truths or keep the commands of God *until* he receives the Spirit. Then he must keep the Ten Commandments, which can be perfectly kept seeing that the power from God is available. Keeping the law keeps a person's justification in force, provides the kind of righteousness that God accepts, and brings about sanctification.

The importance of the Mosaic law (the Ten Commandments) in this system is particularly evident in the redefining of soteriological terms. Repentance, faith, grace, righteousness and sanctification are all defined in such a way that in the end they simply mean "keep the Ten Commandments." The continuance of justification, redemption, and propitiation depends upon the individual's obedience to the Commandments. The protest of Armstrong and his followers that they do not teach a works salvation but that they believe in salvation by faith and grace is absolutely meaningless since they have already given new meaning to these words. Their system is unmistakably a system of works which depends on absolute obedience to the law. They state over and over again that keeping God's Commandments is necessary for eternal life.[115]

Summary and Conclusion

This chapter has attempted to answer some of the major errors of this movement. These key areas affect every significant doctrinal position of the Worldwide Church of God. It has not been possible to answer many of the details. However, it is felt that showing the fallacies of these selected, critical positions in turn reveals the errors of all the others. For example, the teachings in the realm of eschatology were somewhat neglected. However, this is not too serious since both general and individual eschatology depend on the doctrines discussed. The concept of British-Israelism is the foundation on which much of general eschatology is built, while the nature of man, his destiny, and the new birth dictate the views of the resurrection, reward, and punishment. This pattern is true of the other doctrinal areas as well.

In all the areas discussed, it was discovered that the Worldwide Church of God has deviated seriously from biblical truth. Its speculations of British-Israelism are pure fantasy, having no biblical, historical or linguistic basis. Its view of the Godhead is of such a nature that Armstrongism must be classified with the heresies of church history. The concept of God the Father approaches the position of Mormonism; it joins with the Jehovah's Witnesses in its false teaching on the Holy Spirit; and when it gets done presenting its view of Christ, He is no longer God. In fact, there are three Christs, none of which reflect accurately the portrait of Him found in the New Testament.

It has changed the meaning of almost every key word in the doctrine of soteriology and by doing so has removed it from a biblical framework. It has concocted a works salvation which bears no resemblance to the plan of salvation found in the New Testament. In discussing the nature and destiny of man it has restricted the meaning of words and then proceeded to build its structure on those narrow definitions. Furthermore, it was observed that there is no real place given to progressive revelation on this point. The New Testament with its clearer revelation is not allowed to illumine the Old Testament passages which are far less clear.

In all of the areas discussed in this chapter it is most apparent that Herbert Armstrong and his followers have grossly misused the essential element of all Christian theology—words. They have not allowed the verbally inspired words to speak, but have chosen instead to muzzle them and speak for them instead. Certainly this is the basis for all doctrinal error.

It will now be the task of this study to briefly view the hermeneutics of the Worldwide Church of God in an attempt to discover how these false doctrines were arrived at.

The Hermeneutics
of the Worldwide Church of God

The basic responsibility of biblical interpretation is to determine accurately what God has said. The method of interpretation employed will obviously determine what a person thinks God is saying. In analyzing any movement that claims to be Christian, one must carefully scrutinize the principles used in the interpretation of the Scriptures. This, of course, applies to Armstrongism as well as any other group. It is often discovered in the analysis of a group that the philosophy of its interpretation and the practice of it are quite different. This also applies in the case of the Worldwide Church of God.

The Stated Position of Armstrongism

With almost monotonous repetition Armstrongism challenges people to "read their Bible for themselves" and not to let someone else interpret it for them. Readers of Armstrongism's publications and listeners to its radio and television programs are warned to be careful of "Bible helps" since they are often very misleading. Readers are given rules for interpreting the Bible, such as, "check the context carefully," "don't put vague Scriptures first," and "let the Bible interpret itself." Some articles are written for the specific purpose to give instruction concerning Bible study. In one such article, twelve sound principles of Bible interpretation were given from which any Christian could profit greatly by applying them in his own Bible study.[1]

Concerning its own presentation of the Bible, the Worldwide Church of God categorically denies that Herbert Armstrong is the one who does its interpreting.

> So many people write in to THE WORLD TOMORROW and comment how much they enjoy *Mr. Armstrong's interpretation* of the Bible. Over and over again you will hear Mr. Armstrong explain to the radio audience that it is NOT *his interpretation* that is being heard over THE WORLD TOMORROW, *but only* PLAIN BIBLE TRUTH![2]

Most connected with this movement accept such declarations at face value, assuming that what they get is indeed nothing but "plain Bible truth." However, other statements in the literature of Armstrongism, and some actual methods employed shed much light on this claim.

The Role of the Church

Anyone familiar with the literature of the Worldwide Church of God knows that some tremendous assertions are made about the place of this group in God's program and the place of "God's true ministers" in the realm of Bible interpretation. The picture is graphically painted that God has some sacred secrets which He only reveals to His true servants (meaning, of course, those associated with the Worldwide Church of God). There is, to be sure, the biblical truth that both the natural and carnal minds fail to comprehend the truth of God (I Cor. 2:14-3:4), but that is not what is in view here.

> Understand that God reveals prophecy through His true servants . . . Amos 3:7: "Surely the Lord will do nothing, but He revealeth His secret unto His servants the prophets."
> Remember, ONLY God's true servants have come to properly understand prophecy. Others try—by the thousands of hours of preaching and by the tons of printed material. But all for nothing.[3]

This particular article goes on to state that it is "this Work" alone which reveals what is going to take place. Everyone is then encouraged to keep on reading *The Plain Truth.*

In viewing its own role the Worldwide Church of God

also includes the idea that revelation comes through it (revelation here seems to carry the idea of progressive revelation in combination with illumination).

> Seldom, if ever, does a year go by without some vital *new* truth of God's Word and purpose being revealed through this Church and the pages of THE PLAIN TRUTH magazine! To our members and long-time readers, this is a continually *exciting* and *challenging* and PROVABLE fact![4]

Now it should be kept in mind that even though the Church is the subject, in reality Herbert W. Armstrong is being spoken of, for he, in a very real sense, *is* the Church. Who else in that organization would come up with this new truth mentioned above? It is rather improbable that even Garner Ted Armstrong would dare bring in some new interpretation without his father's approval. After being in this movement for ten years, Richard Marson says that new members are quickly taught that they must not disagree with Mr. Armstrong.[5] Concerning Herbert Armstrong's role as interpreter, he states,

> Herbert Armstrong has affected the lives of millions and is looked upon as the interpreter and guide to truth to tens of thousands, who believe he is right.[6]

Chambers makes this observation:

> Armstrongites are taught to interpret Scripture in the light of the writings of Herbert W. Armstrong. It is the common thing for a Worldwide Church of God lecturer, when citing prophecy concerning Israel, to pause and refer his auditors to USBCP for the identity of Israel and the key to prophecy.[7]

After studying the statements and positions of the Worldwide Church of God, it is the conclusion of this writer that the position of Armstrongism bears a great resemblance to that of the Roman Catholic Church. Both of these churches proclaim the authority of the Bible and seem to promote Bible reading among their members. However, both act as the real interpreters of the Bible, and both churches have one man who can and does pronounce authoritatively on matters.

The Interpretive Methods Employed

In studying the doctrines of Armstrongism certain interpretive principles and patterns emerge. These are employed regularly and the results are seen in the doctrines held. The methods actually employed differ noticeably from the principles of interpretation set forth in the literature of Armstrongism. This fact will be seen as these methods of interpretation are detailed.

Extreme Literalism

If a word itself is to mean anything, it must be defined in its normal sense. This is certainly a recognized principle of Bible interpretation. Words must be interpreted literally or one loses the valid base of interpretation. This is not to say that a word might not be taken figuratively if the context demanded it.

In Armstrongism, however, literal interpretation is sometimes taken to an illegitimate extreme in order to prove a point. For example, it identifies the Christmas tree in Jeremiah 10:2-6, and then uses this portion to prove that Christmas trees are condemned by God.

> There is a perfect description of the Christmas tree, termed by the Eternal as "the way of the heathen—the custom of the people." We are commanded not to learn that way or follow it.[8]

However, even a cursory reading of these verses reveals the subject to be the idolatry of Israel and not Christmas trees.

"Knight-jump" Exegesis

In his excellent book *The Four Major Cults,* Anthony Hoekema uses the expression "knight-jump" exegesis to describe an interpretive method of the Jehovah's Witnesses.[9] It is also an apt description of Armstrongism. In chess, the "knight" can jump over other pieces and move a total of three squares forward and to the side, landing on a square of a different color from that on which it started. Armstrongism will sometimes jump from one part of the Bible to another, bypassing contexts, in order to establish some teaching. In his pamphlet on Armstrongism, Paul Wilson records an example of this method in action. In Matthew 19, Jesus told the rich young ruler that he must sell all he had if he were to really keep the commandments. The young man was saddened by these words and Jesus then commented on riches.

> Mr. Armstrong goes on in Matthew 19 to the 25th and 26th verses, and makes a false use of them. He connects the 17th verse to the 25th, as though the disciples said, "Who then can be saved?" when they heard Him refer the young inquirer to the ten commandments. The fact is, however, that in the intervening verses the Lord took up the case of riches as being a hindrance to man's entering the kingdom of God. This was what amazed them, and not, as Mr. Armstrong says, How then can a man be saved if it is a matter of keeping the commandments? That was not the subject, so Mr. Armstrong's use (vs. 26) is in error. It is a twist to make keeping the law for eternal life seem easy, with God's help.[10]

One of the classic examples of the "knight-jump" exegesis in Armstrongism is to be found in the explanation of how the ten "lost" tribes got to England from Canaan. Ephraim (Israel) was taken captive to Assyria. Armstrongism then turns to Hosea 12:1 which states that "Ephraim followeth after the east wind." Since an east wind travels west, therefore, it is reasoned that Ephraim went west from Assyria. Psalm 89:25, speaking of David's throne, says "I will set his hand in the sea." The throne had to be planted west of Assyria in the sea. Jeremiah 3:11, 12 records Jeremiah's commission to Israel: "Go and proclaim these words to the north." So the location of Ephraim is then stated to be toward the north, also west, and in the sea. Isaiah 49:12 says Israel will come from the north and from the west, which means "northwest." Isaiah 49:1 is said to teach that Israel is in the "isles." Jeremiah 31:9, 10 is said to refer to Ephraim and Manasseh: "Hear the word of the Lord, O ye nations and declare it in the isles afar off." Therefore, Israel went afar off to the northwest and dwelt in the isles (coastlines) of the sea.[11] This is the biblical evidence presented by Armstrong-ism to support its position. A refutation is not in order here. The jumping from text to text with complete disregard for contexts is amazing to behold. The combining of totally un-related passages is characteristic of "knight-jump" exegesis.

Misuse of Words

Already in this study, it has been discovered that Arm-strongism characteristically misuses words. In the cases of "sin," "soul," "justification," and others there was an incor-rect restriction placed upon them. In the case of "birth" an entire concept was built on a restriction of the breadth of the Greek language. Armstrongism also misuses words by giving new and unwarranted meanings to them. An example of this is seen in the explanation concerning the worldwide spread of Israel; a misunderstanding of Genesis 28:14.

> The original Hebrew for "spread abroad" means "to break forth."
> This promise places *no limit* on *how far* east, west, north and
> south Jacob's descendants should spread. Thus it indicates they
> would spread around the world.[12]

A study of a lexicon does not suggest any such thing at all. The word has more to do with increase or productivity. The context clearly limits it to the land of Canaan, as does the previous statement of the covenant. The land of Canaan and not the whole world is in view.

Neglect of Biblical Differences

This particular factor is more an error of omission rather than one of commission. In the process of interpreting, the Worldwide Church of God evidences little knowledge of the fact that God has dealt with men differently in the history of mankind. For example, a command given to Moses and Israel would not automatically qualify as a requirement imposed on the saints in the church at Ephesus. The failure to discern some of these differences has its resulting confusion. The Old Testament prophets, especially Ezekiel, are seen directing their messages only to the church of today. The messages of these prophets had almost no importance to the people of their own day. Any valid system of biblical interpretation acknowledges the historical situation of a particular message, though there are differences in an understanding of the full significance of many of these messages. It is, of course, the British-Israelite theory which leads Armstrongism to blur these biblical distinctions. The neglect of such distinctions enables the Worldwide Church of God to wrongly appropriate and apply Old Testament truths in New Testament settings.

Misuse of "Double Fulfillment"

Throughout the literature of the Worldwide Church of God, one reads about "duality" and "dual fulfillment." It is stated that throughout the Scriptures "there is usually a former, typical, and then a final antitypical fulfillment of many prophecies."[13] This concept has given Armstrongism all the latitude it could ever hope for in interpretation. For example, Leviticus 26 is used to construct a fantastically complex doctrine regarding the future, using "dual fulfillment" as a basis.[14] Yet, Leviticus 26 is only speaking of judgment or blessing that will come to the Israelites, depending on their breaking or keeping of the Law. Nowhere in that passage can an unbiased exegete find a second fulfillment relating to the United States and Britain.

It is this kind of abuse that has caused some to shy away from the concept of double fulfillment as a hermeneutical principle. However, it does have a legitimate place in biblical interpretation, because of the principle which is not nearly as flexible as one might think. This principle is clarified by this statement.

> The concept of double reference is not the Pandora's Box of Biblical Hermeneutics as some opponents would claim. It is the failure of many to distinguish application from interpretation that has caused such an accusation to be leveled at the principle. To accept the law of double reference as a legitimate tool for

interpretation of prophecy is not to open the door to all kinds of fanciful notions as to the hidden and allegorical meanings that *might* be alluded to in a prophetic passage.

To speak of the law of double reference is to speak of interpretation, not application. Double reference is not one interpretation and manifold applications. It is one message for two audiences separated in time.[15]

Armstrongism consistently fails to make this distinction and does much of the application, thus abusing a legitimate principle.

Allegorizing

When pressed by a potentially damaging passage of Scripture, the Worldwide Church of God has been known to leave its literal interpretation, which it loudly proclaims, and resort to allegorizing. For example, in the Book of Revelation (6:9-11), the Tribulation martyrs cry out to the Lord to avenge their blood. Now such consciousness after death does not fit into Armstrong theology, so it is said that these martyrs (who died previously) "allegorically are asking how long before the second coming of Christ and the end of the age."[16] One wonders how a person can allegorically cry out.

This same approach to the Scriptures was observed as well in the previous discussion of Lazarus and the rich man. "Abraham's bosom" was taken allegorically, without any justification, to represent Canaan in the millennium.

All evangelicals with a loyalty to the Scriptures realize that the Bible does employ figurative language. Symbolic expressions are used throughout, but the evangelical, whether amillennialist or dispensationalist, strenuously objects when theological bias is allowed to move interpretation into the realm of the absurd. In the example of Lazarus and the rich man, only one with preconceived notions could see an earthly kingdom in these words of the Lord. This is clearly an abuse of the symbolism and figurative language of Scripture.

Summary

Sometimes still other methods are employed to avoid the obvious implications of the Scriptures. For example, the Transfiguration of Christ, with a living Moses and Elijah, is passed off simply as a vision of the disciples. Another interesting procedure is to switch verses around to give the passage a different meaning, as is done to Isaiah 37, placing verse 32 before 31.[17]

After analyzing the interpretations of Armstrongism, one wonders how it can claim to simply be taking the Bible at face value and teaching "plain Bible truth." The wrenching and twisting of Scripture goes on page after page in its writings, defying the hermeneutical principles built on grammatical, contextual and historical considerations.

It is the conclusion of non-Armstrongites that Herbert Armstrong is *the* interpreter for the Worldwide Church of God. After a person has read Armstrongite literature for awhile, he notices a most interesting phenomenon. Unless the reader checks the author of the article he cannot guess who is writing, since all the staff writers sound alike. They have the same basic writing style and they arrive at the same conclusions based on the same argumentation. There is obviously just one mind behind the interpretations.

Conclusion

If it continues its present growth rate, the Worldwide Church of God will become one of the major cults in America and the western world. Already the evangelical church is feeling the presence of this movement and must therefore once again be active in the refutation of damaging heresy. The Church of Jesus Christ cannot afford to be passive or broadminded when both its doctrines and its credibility are called into question. Although this study has not been exhaustive, there are, nevertheless, some definite concluding observations that may be stated.

First, the Worldwide Church of God is rightly classified as a cult. It cannot, in any way, be considered orthodox. It fits precisely the accepted definition of a cult and reflects accurately the attitude of all cultic groups. Despite some very orthodox sounding statements, Armstrongism remains a cult. This judgment is valid because it was discovered that its theological "term-switching" enables it to give the appearance of orthodoxy in many areas, while at the same time holding heretical views.

Second, the Worldwide Church of God is not teaching doctrines that are new and different. Armstrongism has adopted the religious theories and concepts of a variety of religious movements and has successfully blended them together. It is this fact which makes Armstrongism unique, and not, as it claims, that it alone has arrived at the real truth. There is no major teaching held by the Worldwide Church of God that does not somewhere appear in another group. The very late arrival of the system of Armstrongism onto the religious stage in America makes all claims to uniqueness impossible to believe. It has simply put a new cover on an old book and rearranged the chapters considerably.

Third, the Worldwide Church of God has completely rejected the accumulated scholarship of all the centuries of church history. Armstrongism is forced to do this because the Church Fathers and scholars down through church history wrote about and supported many "anti-Armstrong" teachings, such as the Trinity and the Lord's day. Therefore, Irenaeus, Augustine, Calvin, Luther, and others are written off as false brethren doing the work of Satan. With the rejection of such important figures of church history, the claims of Herbert Armstrong for himself become all the more incredible.

Fourth, it must be concluded that this movement is built upon a man. Herbert Armstrong is the founding father, the resident prophet, and the high priest of this church. His mantle will undoubtedly fall one day on his son, Garner Ted, but until that time this man rules his prospering kingdom as the undisputed king.

Fifth, the hermeneutics of the Worldwide Church of God are inconsistent and erroneous in nature. Along with the other cults, it has come to the text of Scripture with preconceived theories seeking validation of its views. The Bible is then forced by illegitimate interpretive methods to say what it does not mean. Armstrongism does not come to the Bible for information, but rather for confirmation.

It has not been the purpose of this study to attack any of the personalities involved in this movement, nor is it the intention now. Perhaps the words of one of Herbert Armstrong's top men sums up the situation well. In writing about others, it seems that Roderick Meredith has painted an accurate portrait of his own leader.

> Many religious "independents" in fact make a "god" out of a pet religious idea or theory that they have concocted—AND WHICH THEY WILL NOT GIVE UP TO SAVE THEIR ETERNAL

LIVES! Such people often have many points of truth because they have departed from the "rut" into which so many religious denominations have fallen, but they are so filled with spiritual *pride* and VANITY that they are totally unable to see the obvious and in many cases the ridiculous error into which they themselves have fallen!

They have made a veritable "god" out of their pet religious theory—and they serve that god zealously and unremitingly![1]

Nothing needs to be added to this analysis.

Appendix

It has been the pattern in the past for a cult to experience some splinter movements at the death of its founder. History has shown that while one main body may remain, several other groups will form also. In the case of the Worldwide Church of God (WCG) this fragmentation began before the death of its founder, Herbert W. Armstrong (HWA). Since the founding of the WCG in 1934, HWA ruled without any challenge to his authority, teachings or life style. But after almost four decades of dictatorial rule things began to change.

The Troubled Years of 1972-1974

Towards the end of 1973 dissention of major proportions exploded within the WCG. The revolt against the Armstrongs by some of the leaders within the WCG came as a result of certain specific charges leveled against the two Armstrongs. First, it was charged that Garner Ted Armstrong (GTA) had been engaging in "profoundly immoral activities" over a period of years. The dissident leaders further accused HWA and other high ranking leaders of concealing and covering up the alleged adultery of GTA (Los Angeles *Times,* February 24, 1974). The alleged adulterous conduct of the younger Armstrong is said to be the main reason for disfellowshiping him early in 1972. GTA was later declared to be repentant and was restored four months later to his former position. HWA soon after appointed him as the "anointed heir." But it was claimed by some that GTA still had his "problem" (Chicago *Sun Times,* May 31, 1974).

A second charge was that the Armstrongs and other leading officials in the church were squandering the church's money with their luxurious style of living. The dissidents cited the three jets and one propjet which were being leased at a reported four million dollars a year. These planes were used to fly the Armstrongs all over the world. At least three mansions were at the disposal of the Armstrongs. This luxurious life style was especially galling to many in the movement in light of several "urgent" appeals by HWA to the membership for money. Other unnecessary expenses, such as the multi-million dollar auditorium on the Pasadena campus, were cited.

A third charge was that the Armstrongs ruled the church as dictators and that they were inflexible in the discussion of doctrine and practice. The dissidents claimed that there was no allowance for differences. They focused upon the areas of divorce and remarriage and the multiple tithe.

The Armstrongs responded to these accusations by charging that the rebellious ministers were self-seeking, desiring to line their own pockets and establish their own congregations. HWA viewed the revolt as an all-out war by Satan against the church.

The open revolt against the Armstrongs was not a sudden thing. Internal strife had been present since early 1972. However, open division occurred in November 1973 with the resignations of important WCG leaders. Six ministers had resigned by February of 1974. The defection of Alfred Carrozzo, once director of ministers for the western half of the United States, shook the movement. The revolt seemed ready to engulf the entire church as the six ministers prepared an angry twelve-page letter for the information of the membership of the WCG. Sunday, February 24th, HWA cut short a visit to the Philippines and hurried home to stem the tide. Monday, the 25th, GTA announced the suspension of twenty ministers. He also announced that the sabbath services of March 2nd were canceled and the day was set aside for fasting and prayer. The next sabbath (March 9th) was declared a day of solemn assembly.

Resignations also came from two church vice-presidents, David Antion and Albert Portune. The revolt seemed to be spreading. (Later, these two retracted their resignations and took a two-month leave of absence.)

HWA arrived back in the United States and spoke to some 2,000 members at Pasadena. He took a hard line attitude, calling the defection from the WCG a work of Satan. However, the very next week a new association was formed by thirty-five former ministers of the WCG. This splinter group took the name of The Associated Churches of God. This group which was formed in Washington, D.C., was estimated to have between 2,000 and 2,500 former members of the WCG. These had obtained their goal of liberation from the Armstrongs.

This schism hurt the WCG in money, membership and prestige. The damage to the WCG would have been greater if HWA had not been there to stem the tide. When the revolt was over, other ministers had left the WCG and perhaps around 5,000 members departed the church during those years.

The Critical Years of 1977-1980

In the years that followed the revolt of the early 1970s, HWA and GTA continued to rule the church, with HWA being the dominant force. Serious charges of misconduct were periodically raised. Continuing charges of immoral conduct and luxurious living were leveled against GTA. These charges against GTA, and some against HWA, have been published in books, pamphlets and "open letters." *The Broadway to Armageddon* (1977), by William Hinson, *Armstrongism: Religion or Rip-Off?* (1977), by Marion McNair and *Herbert Armstrong's Tangled Web* (1980), by David Robinson are among the most devastating works by former WCG members. Yet, in spite of these revealing books, thousands still see HWA as God's apostle.

In early 1977, HWA was married again after being a widower for some ten years. In his mid-eighties, HWA married Ramona Martin (in her thirties). HWA reported on his marriage in the July 1977 issue of *The Plain Truth*. This marriage lasted for five years and then HWA filed for divorce. As usual, HWA was able to use the Bible to explain away his divorce, likening it to God's divorce of Israel in the Old Testament (*The Plain Truth*, May 1982).

Undoubtedly the most significant incident during the late 1970s was the excommunication of GTA by his father HWA. GTA's influence in the church had begun to grow and he began making some changes. In the power struggle that followed, HWA ousted him from his executive positions in the church and Ambassador College, the church's educational arm. In early 1978 GTA was ordered to take a leave of absence to "regain his spirituality." He was to remain in isolation and speak to no one during this time. However, GTA spoke out in protest against the treatment he received, giving his side of the story to both the media and to church members. GTA accused the church leadership of lavish spending and ruling by means of fear. HWA responded by excommunicating GTA and warning all members of the WCG to have no dealings with him. Thus the separation between father and son was complete, with no apparent hope of any kind of reconciliation (Pasadena *Star News*, June 29, 1978).

The very next month GTA formed a new church, named the Church of God International. This splinter group was located in Tyler, Texas (Pasadena *Star News*, July 30, 1978). HWA warned members of his church not to follow his ousted son (Los Angeles *Times*, August 5, 1978). Some did go with the new group and GTA began broadcasting immediately, beginning on a San Antonio station.

The split with GTA was not the only major problem faced by HWA and his church. In January of 1979 the State of California filed suit against the WCG. The attorney general's office charged HWA and his chief aide, Stanley Rader, with "pilfering" the church assets at the rate of "several million dollars a year" and destroying vital financial documents. This suit was filed by the attorney general with six co-plaintiffs, all former members of the WCG (Los Angeles *Times*, January 4, 1979). A temporary receiver was ordered to take possession and control of the WCG, and was to conduct a thorough audit and review all allegations. The WCG countersued, and a legal battle was on. The emotional issue of church-state relations and First Amendment rights quickly entered the picture. The WCG planned to move from California to Arizona — away from the "persecution" by the state (Los Angeles *Times*, January 22, 1979). HWA took out full-page ads in large newspapers in a counterattack. HWA told his followers that this was another all-out attack by Satan against the true church. This action by the State of California did cause many religious groups to rally around the WCG, fearing that the government was indeed overstepping its authority. In October of 1980 the State of California dropped its two-year investigation into the internal affairs of the WCG. The WCG had seemingly weathered another storm.

The Future of the Worldwide Church of God

The WCG has overcome its setbacks and experienced growth again. According to *Christianity Today* (August 6, 1982), the church's income was up to $108 million in 1981. *The Plain Truth* magazine climbed to a very healthy 4.3 million copies monthly in 1981. The World Tomorrow broadcast, which features HWA, was on 100 radio and 144 television stations. Growth was seen in its congregations, colleges and mailing lists. Thousands of new people are annually being reached with the gospel according to Armstrong.

The future leadership of the WCG is a question. Normally, GTA would have been the heir to his father's religious empire. That seems unlikely now. Perhaps the WCG will follow the lead of other groups who lost their founder-leader and establish a ruling hierarchy.

It should be noted that in all the turmoil, defections and charges, few changes doctrinally have taken place. Modifications have occured in the WCG regarding medical science, divorce and remarriage, the second and third tithes, women's clothing and some other lesser issues. The theory of British-Israelism continues to be deemphasized, and is not preached as a cornerstone doctrine any longer. The nineteen-year time cycles and other predictions relating to end-time events which were to occur between 1972 and 1975 are, needless to say, absent from current WCG teachings (see pages 65-68). One slight doctrinal adjustment that should be noted is in regards to the spirit of man. Joseph Hopkins reported on this in the April 15, 1977 publication of *Christianity Today*.

> Herbert W. Armstrong had previously taught that man's nature is essentially no different from that of animals. But a dozen years ago he gained the insight that human beings have a capacity for spiritual communion, noble aspiration, moral sensitivity, and creativity that distinguishes them from other creatures. The "spirit in man" concept is midway between the mechanistic view of human nature and the traditional Christian belief that man has an "immortal soul" that survives physical death. The latter belief is denied in the WCG.

At this point in time the WCG continues to grow and is therefore a force that the orthodox church must contend with. Many in the movement are discontent but are kept there by legalism and fear. Others who have departed the WCG have left it but still have not found the truth. To all these the orthodox church must share the liberating truth of salvation by faith alone in the finished work of Jesus Christ.

Paul N. Benware, 1984.

Notes

Chapter 1

1. Roderick Meredith, "The True Church—Where Is It?" *The Plain Truth* (March, 1963), p. 44.

2. Herman L. Hoeh, *A True History of the True Church* (Pasadena: Ambassador College Press, 1959), p. 28.

3. Herbert Armstrong, *Just What Do You Mean . . . Kingdom of God?* (Pasadena: Ambassador College Press, 1962), p. 3; also cf. *The Autobiography of Herbert W. Armstrong* (Pasadena: Ambassador College Press, 1967), p. 503.

4. Herbert Armstrong, *The Book of Revelation Unveiled at Last* (Pasadena: Ambassador College Press, 1959), p. 4.

5. Gordon Lewis, *Confronting the Cults* (Philadelphia: Presbyterian and Reformed Publishing Company, 1966), p. 3.

6. Walter R. Martin, *The Kingdom of the Cults* (Minneapolis, Minn.: Bethany Fellowship, Inc., 1970), p. 18. Also note A. Hoekema, *The Four Major Cults* (Grand Rapids: Wm. B. Eerdmans Publishing Co., 1970), pp. 373 ff. where several other traits are suggested including a tendency to major on minor points, a tendency towards perfectionism and a disregard of church history.

7. Ibid., p. 20.

8. Ibid., p. 24.

9. Russell Spittler, *Cults and Isms* (Grand Rapids: Baker Book House, 1962), p. 16.

10. Martin, *Kingdom of the Cults*, p. 25.

11. Ibid.

12. Ibid., p. 26.

13. *This is the Worldwide Church of God* (Pasadena: Ambassador College Press, 1972), p. 6.

14. Ibid., p. 15.

15. Ibid., p. 19. They claim to be reaching 150 million people through the various forms of mass media.

16. Ibid., p. 15. Armstrongism states that the programs are being carried on about 400 radio and television stations with more than 50 million watts of power weekly.

17. Haddon W. Robinson, "The Impact of Religious Radio and

Television Programs on American Life," *Bibliotheca Sacra,* Vol. 123, No. 490 (April, 1966), pp. 124-35.

18. Ibid., p. 129.

19. Charles F. DeLoach, *The Armstrong Error* (Plainfield, New Jersey: Logos International, 1970), p. 12.

20. William C. Martin, "The God-Hucksters of Radio," *The Atlantic Monthly* (June, 1970), p. 54.

21. *This is the Worldwide Church of God,* p. 20.

22. Richard A. Marson, *The Marson Report Concerning Herbert W. Armstrong* (Seattle: The Ashley-Calvin Press, 1970), p. 6.

23. The circulation of *The Plain Truth* reached 2,821,000 in March, 1973. Advertising space has been purchased by the Worldwide Church of God in *T.V. Guide* and other magazines with large circulations in order to offer free subscriptions to *The Plain Truth.*

24. DeLoach, *The Armstrong Error,* p. 17.

25. *This is the Worldwide Church of God,* p. 17.

26. Marson, *The Marson Report Concerning Herbert W. Armstrong,* p. 14.

27. Joseph Hopkins, "Herbert W. Armstrong," *Christianity Today,* Vol. XVI, No. 6 (December 17, 1971), p. 7.

28. Ibid.

29. Marson, *The Marson Report Concerning Herbert W. Armstrong,* p. 6.

30. Ibid., p. 12.

31. Ibid., p. 15. A recent estimate places the income at around 55 million dollars. Leslie Tarr, "Herbert W. Armstrong: Does He Really Have the Plain Truth?" *Moody Monthly,* September, 1972, p. 25. This estimate was confirmed as fairly accurate in a personal interview with Mr. Les Stocker of Ambassador College, Pasadena, Calif., January, 1973. In the same interview a figure of eighty percent was considered more accurate for the percentage of the income from tithing members.

Chapter 2

1. Herbert W. Armstrong, *The Autobiography of Herbert W. Armstrong* (Pasadena: Ambassador College Press, 1967), pp. 17-30.

2. Ibid., p. 33.

3. Ibid., p. 75.

4. Ibid., p. 76.

5. Ibid., pp. 78, 79.

6. Ibid., p. 82.

7. Ibid., p. 26.

8. Ibid., p. 297.

9. Ibid., pp. 298, 299.

10. Ibid., p. 492.

11. Letter to *Plain Truth* readers. November 21, 1966.

12. *This is Ambassador College* (Pasadena: Ambassador College Press, 1969), p. 60.

13. "Preacher Will Return to T.V.," *Los Angeles Times* (June 3, 1972), 1. 30.

14. "The Ambassador College Radio Studio," *Tomorrow's World* (February, 1971), p. 25.

15. "Religious News," *Christianity Today*, XVI, No. 15 (April 14, 1972), p. 39.

16. Armstrong, *Autobiography*, p. 376.

17. Letter to *Plain Truth* readers, November 24, 1967.

18. Ibid.

19. Ibid.

20. "Religious News," *Christianity Today*, p. 39.

21. Armstrong, *Autobiography*, pp. 207, 208.

22. Herbert W. Armstrong, "No! I Never Was a 'Jehovah's Witness,' or a Seventh-day Adventist!," *The Plain Truth* (July, 1953), p. 5.

23. Harry Lowe, *Radio Church of God* (Mountain View, California: Pacific Press Publishing Association, 1970), pp. 18, 19. The Church of God (Seventh-day) moved its headquarters to Denver, Colorado in 1972.

24. Letter to Robert L. Odom, March 11, 1953, cited by Harry Lowe, *Radio Church of God*, p. 22.

25. Letter from Faith Ling, Sec.-Treas. of the Bible Advocate Press, January 6, 1972.

26. Lowe, *Radio Church of God*, pp. 23, 24.

27. Herbert Armstrong in a Circular letter, cited by Paul Wilson, *The Armstrong Heresy* (Denver: Wilson Foundation, n.d.), p. 4.

28. Herman Hoeh, *A True History of the True Church*, p. 26.

29. Herbert Armstrong, *The United States and British Commonwealth in Prophecy* (Pasadena: Ambassador College, 1967), p. 212.

30. Armstrong, *Autobiography*, p. 503.

31. Ibid., p. 505.

32. Herbert Armstrong, *1975 in Prophecy* (Pasadena: Ambassador College Press, 1957), p. 20.

33. Herbert Armstrong, "Personal from Herbert W. Armstrong," *Tomorrow's World* (February, 1972), p. 1.

34. Armstrong, *Autobiography*, pp. 400, 407.

35. Roger R. Chambers, *The Plain Truth About Armstrongism* (Grand Rapids: Baker Book House, 1972), p. 17.

36. Armstrong, *Autobiography*, p. 338.

37. William F. Dankenbring, "Does It Matter Which Day You Keep?" *Tomorrow's World* (March, 1971), p. 36.

38. "Did Christ Change the Sabbath?" *Signs of the Times* (August, 1966), p. 17.

39. H. W. Armstrong, *Which Day is the Christian Sabbath?* (Pasadena: Ambassador College Press, 1971), p. 35.

40. O. A. Johnson, cited by Norman F. Douty, *Another Look at Seventh-day Adventism* (Grand Rapids: Baker Book House, 1962), p. 78.

41. Herbert Armstrong, *The Mark of the Beast* (Pasadena: Ambassador College Press, 1957), pp. 10, 11.

42. *Advent Review Extra* (August, 1850), cited by D. M. Canright, *Seventh-day Adventism Renounced* (Chicago: Fleming H. Revell, 1889), p. 43.

43. *Seventh-day Adventists Answer Questions on Doctrine* (Washington, D.C.: Review and Herald Publishing Association, 1957), pp. 197 ff.

44. Eugene Walter, "The Apostle Paul—Commandment Breaker, or Commandment Keeper?" *Tomorrow's World* (January, 1972), p. 25.

45. *Questions on Doctrine*, p. 121.

46. Roderick C. Meredith, *The Ten Commandments* (Pasadena: Ambassador College Press, 1968), p. 17.

47. W. H. Branson, *Drama of the Ages* (Nashville: Southern Publishing Association, 1963), pp. 308, 309.

48. Herbert Armstrong, "Were the Ten Commandments Nailed to the Cross?" *The Plain Truth* (May, 1962), p. 8.

49. *Questions on Doctrine*, pp. 129, 130.

50. Garner Ted Armstrong, "Do You Have an Immortal Soul?" Reprint No. 290, Ambassador College Press, 1971, p. 2.

51. *Questions on Doctrine*, p. 513.

52. Garner Ted Armstrong, "Immortal Soul?," p. 3.

53. *Questions on Doctrine*, p. 515.

54. Garner Ted Armstrong, "Immortal Soul?," p. 8.

55. *Questions on Doctrine*, p. 518.

56. Garner Ted Armstrong, "What is Death?" Reprint No. 870, Ambassador College Press, 1970, pp. 4, 7.

57. LeRoy Froom, *The Conditionalist Faith of Our Fathers*, Vol. 1 (Washington, D.C.: The Review and Herald Publishing Association, 1966), p. 467.

58. Garner Ted Armstrong, "Who—What—Was Jesus Before His Human Birth?" Reprint No. 370, Ambassador College Press, 1957, p. 2.

59. *Questions on Doctrine*, p. 63.

60. Herbert Armstrong, *Just What Do You Mean . . . Born Again?* (Pasadena: Ambassador College Press, 1962), pp. 8, 13, 14.

61. "Fundamental Beliefs," cited by Norman Douty, *Another Look at Seventh-day Adventism*, pp. 71, 72.

62. H. W. Armstrong, *Just What Do You Mean . . . Born Again?* p. 19.

63. *Let God Be True* (Brooklyn: The Watchtower Bible and Tract Society, 1952), p. 101.

64. G. Geis, "The God Family: Open or Closed?" *Tomorrow's World* (September, 1970), p. 30.

65. *Let God Be True*, p. 108.

66. Herbert Armstrong, "Why Christ Died—and Rose Again!" *Tomorrow's World* (March, 1970), p. 8.

67. *Let God Be True*, p. 40.

68. Armstrong, *Just What Do You Mean . . . Born Again?* p. 12.

69. Herbert Armstrong, *Lazarus and the Rich Man* (Pasadena: Radio Church of God, 1953), p. 11.

70. *Let God Be True*, p. 92.

71. David Jon Hill, "Why is God the Father Called a Father?" *Tomorrow's World* (September, 1970), p. 28.

72. *From Paradise Lost to Paradise Regained* (Brooklyn: Watchtower Bible and Tract Society, 1958), p. 229.

73. Hill, "Why is God the Father Called a Father?" p. 27.

74. James E. Talmage, *A Study of the Articles of Faith* (17th ed.; Salt Lake City: The Church of the Latter-day Saints, 1937), p. 430.

75. David Hill and Robert Kuhn, "Why Does God Hide Himself?" *Tomorrow's World* (December, 1969), p. 11.

76. Talmage, *Articles of Faith*, p. 69.

77. Armstrong, *Autobiography*, pp. 502, 503.

78. Talmage, *Articles of Faith*, pp. 203, 204.

79. Herbert W. Armstrong, "What is the True Gospel?" *Tomorrow's World* (January, 1970), p. 7.

80. Statement made by Joseph Smith on June 16, 1844. Reproduced in *Teachings of the Prophet Joseph Smith*, ed. Joseph Fielding Smith (Salt Lake City, Utah: Deseret Book Co., 1970), p. 372.

81. Herbert W. Armstrong, *The United States and British Commonwealth in Prophecy* (Pasadena: Ambassador College Press, 1967), p. 80.

82. J. H. Allen, *Judah's Sceptre and Joseph's Birthright* (17th ed.; Boston: A. A. Beauchamp, 1943), p. 66.

83. Armstrong, *USBCP*, p. 82.

84. Allen, *Judah's Sceptre*, p. 71.

85. Armstrong, *USBCP*, pp. 35, 36.

86. Allen, *Judah's Sceptre*, p. 36.

87. Armstrong, *USBCP*, pp. 95, 96.

88. Allen, *Judah's Sceptre*, p. 166.

89. Armstrong, *USBCP*, pp. 95, 96.

90. Allen, *Judah's Sceptre*, pp. 166, 167.

Chapter 3

1. Garner Ted Armstrong, "How Much of the Bible Should You Reject?" *Tomorrow's World* (March, 1971), p. 6.

2. Herbert Armstrong, *Which Day is the Christian Sabbath?* (Pasadena: Ambassador College Press, 1972), p. 18.

3. Herman Hoeh, "Do We Have the Complete Bible?" Reprint No. 590 (Pasadena: Ambassador College Press), 1972, p. 6.

4. L. L. Grabbe, "Daniel—Battleground of Biblical Criticism," *Tomorrow's World* (January, 1971), p. 38.

5. Brian Knowles, "How You Can Understand Prophecy and Prophetic Terminology," *Tomorrow's World* (January, 1972), p. 18.

6. R. L. Kuhn, "How to Understand Prophecy," *Tomorrow's World* (January, 1972), p. 41.

7. Garner Ted Armstrong, "Seven Proofs God Exists," *Tomorrow's World* (October, 1971), p. 9.

8. Herbert W. Armstrong, *Does God Exist?* (Pasadena: Ambassador College Press, 1957), p. 2.

9. David Jon Hill, "Why is God the Father Called a Father?" *Tomorrow's World* (September, 1970), p. 27.

10. Roderick Meredith, *The Ten Commandments* (Pasadena: Ambassador College Press, 1968), pp. 49, 50.

11. "Answers to Questions," *Tomorrow's World* (November, 1970), p. 23.

12. J. O. Grabbe, "Only One God is God!" *Tomorrow's World* (March, 1972), p. 21.

13. Garner Ted Armstrong, "Don't Let Life Happen!" *Tomorrow's World* (March, 1970), p. 10.

14. Meredith, *Ten Commandments,* pp. 15, 49.

15. Meredith, *Ten Commandments,* p. 48.

16. B. McDowell, "Is the Holy Spirit a Person?" *Tomorrow's World* (September, 1970), p. 31.

17. Hill, "Why is God the Father Called a Father?" p. 27.

18. Ibid., p. 24.

19. Herbert Armstrong, *Predestination—Does the Bible Teach It?* (Pasadena: Ambassador College Press, 1957), pp. 18-21.

20. McDowell, "Is the Holy Spirit a Person?" p. 32.

21. Hill, "Why is God the Father Called a Father?" p. 28.

22. Herbert W. Armstrong, *Just What Do You Mean . . . Born Again?* (Pasadena: Ambassador College Press, 1962), p. 20.

23. David Hill and Robert Kuhn, "Why Does God Hide Himself?" *Tomorrow's World* (December, 1969), p. 32.

24. Herbert W. Armstrong, "Why Christ Died—and Rose Again!" *Tomorrow's World* (March, 1970), p. 5.

25. Herbert W. Armstrong, "Is Jesus God?" Reprint No. 370, Ambassador College Press, 1957, pp. 4, 6.

26. H. W. Armstrong, "Why Christ Died—and Rose Again!" p. 6.

27. Herbert W. Armstrong, "Millions Do not Know What Christ Really Was!" *The Plain Truth* (November, 1963), pp. 11, 12.

28. Herbert W. Armstrong, "Why Christ Died—and Rose Again!" *The Plain Truth* (April, 1963), p. 10.

29. Ibid.

30. H. W. Armstrong, "Millions Do Not Know," p. 10.

31. Hill, "Why is God the Father Called a Father?" p. 27.

32. Ibid.

33. Garner Ted Armstrong, "Who—What—Was Jesus Before His Human Birth?" Reprint No. 370, Ambassador College Press, 1957, p. 3.

34. Herbert W. Armstrong, "Was Jesus Christ Born Again?" *The Plain Truth* (February, 1963), pp. 8, 9.

35. Herbert W. Armstrong, "Why Christ Died—and Rose Again?" *Tomorrow's World* (March, 1970), p. 8.

36. Herbert W. Armstrong, *All About Water Baptism* (Pasadena: Ambassador College Press, 1972), p. 2.

37. Herbert W. Armstrong, *The Resurrection Was Not on Sunday!* (Pasadena: Ambassador College Press, 1952), p. 10.

38. H. W. Armstrong, "Why Christ Died . . . and Rose Again!" p. 7.

39. H. W. Armstrong, *The Resurrection Was Not on Sunday!* p. 10.

40. H. W. Armstrong, *Just What Do You Mean . . . Born Again?* p. 12.

41. H. W. Armstrong, "Why Christ Died . . . and Rose Again!" p. 8.

42. H. W. Armstrong, *Just What Do You Mean . . . Born Again?* p. 13.

43. Herbert W. Armstrong, "What Do You Mean . . . 'The Unpardonable Sin'?" *Tomorrow's World* (July, 1971), p. 1.

44. Herbert W. Armstrong, "Spiritism: Fraud or Fact?," Reprint No. 196, Ambassador College Press, 1955, p. 1.

45. Herbert W. Armstrong, "Did God Create a Devil?" Reprint No. 440, Ambassador College Press, 1971, pp. 1-3.

46. Garner Ted Armstrong, "What is Satan's Fate?" Reprint No. 440, Ambassador College Press, 1971, pp. 4-8.

47. H. W. Armstrong, "Spiritism," pp. 1-4.

48. Herbert W. Armstrong, *Why Were You Born?* (Pasadena: Ambassador College Press, 1957), p. 10.

49. Hill and Kuhn, "Why Does God Hide Himself?" p. 11.

50. H. W. Armstrong, "Why Were You Born?" p. 8.

51. Hill and Kuhn, "Why Does God Hide Himself?" p. 11.

52. Garner Ted Armstrong, "Do You Have an Immortal Soul?" Reprint No. 290, Ambassador College Press, 1971, p. 3.

53. Ibid., pp. 2, 7.

54. Ibid., p. 8.

55. Ibid., p. 2.

56. Herbert W. Armstrong, "What is the True Gospel?" *Tomorrow's World* (January, 1970), p. 7.

57. Hill and Kuhn, "Why Does God Hide Himself?," p. 34.

58. Garner Ted Armstrong, "What is Death?," Reprint No. 870, Ambassador College Press, 1970, p. 6.

59. Armstrong, "Immortality," p. 7.

60. Meredith, *The Ten Commandments*, p. 10.

61. H. W. Armstrong, "What Do You Mean . . . 'The Unpardonable Sin'?" pp. 42-48.

62. Hill and Kuhn, "Why Does God Hide Himself?" p. 11.

63. H. W. Armstrong, "What Do You Mean—'The Unpardonable Sin'?" pp. 42-48.

64. H. W. Armstrong, "What Do You Mean . . . the 'Unpardonable Sin'?" p. 45.

65. Leslie McCullough, "Just What Do You Mean—Repentance?" *Tomorrow's World* (August, 1971), p. 4.

66. Herbert W. Armstrong, "What Kind of Faith is Required for Salvation?" *Tomorrow's World* (August, 1971), p. 4.

67. H. W. Armstrong, *All About Water Baptism*, p. 8.

68. Ibid., pp. 18, 19.

69. Armstrong, *All About Water Baptism*, pp. 7, 8.

70. Herbert W. Armstrong, "Was Jesus Christ Born Again?" *The Plain Truth* (February, 1963), p. 40.

71. Ibid.

72. H. W. Armstrong, "What Do You Mean . . . 'Unpardonable Sin'?" p. 42.

73. Ibid.

74. H. W. Armstrong, *Why Were You Born?* p. 14.

75. H. W. Armstrong, "What Do You Mean . . . 'Unpardonable Sin'?" p. 41.

76. H. W. Armstrong, "What Kind of Faith?" p. 41.

77. Geis, "The God Family: Open or Closed?" p. 30.

78. Herbert W. Armstrong, "The Wonderful World Tomorrow," *Tomorrow's World* (September, 1971), p. 2.

79. Herman Hoeh, *A True History of the True Church* (Pasadena: Ambassador College Press, 1959), p. 3.

80. Roderick Meredith, "The True Church—Where is It?" *The Plain Truth* (March, 1963), pp. 43, 45.

81. Garner Ted Armstrong, "Why a Church?" *The Plain Truth* (August, 1962), p. 27.

82. Herbert W. Armstrong, "Just What is The Church?" *Tomorrow's World* (July, 1970), pp. 3, 4.

83. Ibid., p. 6.

84. Armstrong, *All About Water Baptism*, p. 21.

85. Herbert W. Armstrong, "How Often Should We Partake of the Lord's Supper?" *Tomorrow's World* (March, 1971), p. 5.

86. Meredith, "The True Church—Where is It?" pp. 44, 45.

87. For support of this position see Robert L. Saucy, *The Church in God's Program* (Chicago: Moody Press, 1972), p. 34.

88. Herbert W. Armstrong, *The United States and British Commonwealth in Prophecy* (Pasadena: Ambassador College Press, 1967), p. 132. (Hereinafter referred to as *USBCP*.)

89. Harry W. Lowe, *Radio Church of God* (Mountain View, Calif.: Pacific Press Publishing Association, 1970), p. 10.

90. Ibid., p. 11.

91. Ibid., p. 15.

92. Ibid., p. 135.

93. Herbert W. Armstrong, "The 19-year Time Cycles—What Hap-

pened January 7—What My Commission Is!" *Tomorrow's World* (February, 1972), p. 1.

94. Herbert W. Armstrong, *1975 in Prophecy* (Pasadena: Ambassador College Press, 1952), p. 10.

95. Ibid., p. 20.

96. Herbert W. Armstrong, *Just What Do You Mean . . . Kingdom of God?* (Pasadena: Ambassador College Press, 1962), p. 7.

97. H. W. Armstrong, *USBCP*, p. 134.

98. Ibid., p. 184.

99. Ibid., p. 185.

100. Hoeh, *A True History of the True Church*, p. 27.

101. Herbert W. Armstrong, *The Book of Revelation Unveiled at Last!* (Pasadena: Radio Church of God, 1959), p. 22.

102. H. W. Armstrong and G. T. Armstrong, *The Wonderful World Tomorrow* (Pasadena: Ambassador College Press, 1966), p. 40.

103. H. W. Armstrong, *1975 in Prophecy*, pp. 27, 28.

104. Albert Portune, "Will There Be a Secret Rapture?" *The Plain Truth* (February, 1963), p. 45.

105. Ibid., p. 46.

106. Armstrong, *Revelation Unveiled*, p. 14.

107. Ibid., p. 18.

108. H. W. Armstrong, *1975 in Prophecy*, p. 25.

109. Ibid., p. 31.

110. Herbert W. Armstrong, "Why Were You Born?" *The Plain Truth* (August, 1972), p. 16.

111. Armstrong, *1975 in Prophecy*, p. 31.

112. C. Paul Meredith, "If You Die . . . Will You Live Again?" Reprint No. 270, Ambassador College Press, 1971, p. 7.

113. Armstrong and Armstrong, *Wonderful World Tomorrow*, p. 43.

114. Gary Alexander, "The Greening of the World," *Tomorrow's World* (August, 1971), p. 20.

115. Herbert W. Armstrong, "The Wonderful World Tomorrow," *Tomorrow's World* (September, 1971), p. 2.

116. Armstrong and Armstrong, *Wonderful World Tomorrow*, p. 60.

117. Meredith, "If You Die . . . Will You Life Again?" p. 7.

118. Ibid.

119. Ibid., pp. 6, 7.

120. Herbert W. Armstrong, "How Would Jesus Vote for President?" *The Plain Truth* (October, 1964), pp. 25-30.

121. Herbert W. Armstrong, *Does God Heal Today?* (Pasadena: Ambassador College Press, 1952), p. 6. In an interview with Mr. Les Stocker of Ambassador College, Pasadena, California, January, 1973, the view was presented that the use of medicines is viewed as a lack of faith. However, members are not prohibited by the Church from seeking medical help.

Chapter 4

1. Herbert W. Armstrong, *The United States and British Commonwealth in Prophecy* (Pasadena: Ambassador College Press, 1967), p. 4. (Hereinafter referred to as *USBCP*).

2. Ibid., p. 26.

3. Ibid., p. 30.

4. Ibid., pp. 35, 36.

5. Ibid., p. 83.

6. Ibid., p. 86.

7. Ibid., p. 68.

8. Ibid., pp. 88, 89.

9. Ibid., p. 89.

10. Ibid., p. 114.

11. Ibid., pp. 115, 116.

12. Ibid., pp. 117, 118.

13. Ibid., p. 96.

14. Ibid., pp. 96, 97.

15. Ibid., pp. 118, 121, 122.

16. "Jew," *The Jewish Encyclopedia*, 1904, VII, 174. See also, Richard Trench, *Synonyms of the New Testament* (Grand Rapids: Wm. B. Eerdmans Publishing Co., 1953), pp. 137-143.

17. Von Rad, "Ἰσραήλ. Israel, Judah and Hebrews in the Old Testament," *Theological Dictionary of the New Testament*, ed. by G. Kittel, trans. by G. Bromiley, Vol. III (Grand Rapids: Wm. B. Eerdmans Publishing Co., 1965), p. 357.

18. K. G. Kuhn, "Ἰσραήλ, Ιουδαῖος, Εβραῖος in Jewish Literature After the Old Testament," *Theological Dictionary of the New Testament*, ed. by G. Kittel, trans. by G. Bromiley, Vol. III (Grand Rapids: Wm. B. Eerdmans Publishing Co., 1965), p. 359.

19. David Baron, *The History of the Ten "Lost" Tribes* (London: Morgan and Scott Ld., 1915), pp. 36, 37.

20. Roger Chambers, *The Plain Truth About Armstrongism* (Grand Rapids: Baker Book House, 1972), p. 70.

21. Ibid., p. 51.

22. Armstrongism very clearly teaches that there were no members of the Northern Kingdom in the South. Compare *USBCP*, p. 89.

23. Ibid., p. 53.

24. *Ancient Near Eastern Texts Relating to the Old Testament*, ed. by James B. Pritchard, trans. by A. L. Oppenheim, (2nd ed.; Princeton, New Jersey: Princeton University Press, 1955), pp. 284, 285.

25. D. Winton Thomas, ed., *Documents from Old Testament Times*, Harper Torchbooks, (New York: Harper and Row, 1961), p. 59.

26. It is clear that Armstrongism believes in a 100 percent depopulation of the Northern Kingdom. The Samaritans, who came to live in that land, are said to be gentiles and in no sense are they a racial mixture. Furthermore, it is held that only one Israelite, a priest, ever returned to the land. Compare *USBCP*, pp. 86-89.

27. In his book cited above, Roger Chambers has an interesting word on the logistics of deportation, pointing out that attempting to move entire nations with millions of people over hundreds of miles would present Assyria with an overwhelming problem (pp. 77-79).

28. In 3:1-15 the phrase "house of Israel" is used several times. In 4:4-6 the terms "house of Israel" and "house of Judah" are both used indicating that each primarily looks at its respective kingdom. Thus, if the term is so used in chapter 3, the indication is that Ezekiel had a ministry to both groups of exiles.

29. Baron, *History of the Ten "Lost" Tribes*, p. 30.

30. Walter Martin, *The Kingdom of the Cults* (Minneapolis: Bethany Fellowship, Inc., 1969), p. 304.

31. Chambers, *The Plain Truth About Armstrongism*, p. 79.

32. John F. Walvoord, *The Millennial Kingdom* (Findlay, Ohio: Dunham Publishing Company, 1963), pp. 201, 202.

33. Herbert Armstrong, ed. *Ambassador College Correspondence Course,* Lesson 8, (Pasadena: Ambassador College Press, 1972), pp. 5-9.

34. Ibid., p. 5.

35. Robert B. Girdlestone, *Synonyms of the Old Testament* (Grand Rapids: Wm. B. Eerdmans Publishing Company, 1956), p. 19.

36. August H. Strong, *Systematic Theology* (Old Tappan, New Jersey: Fleming H. Revell Company, 1906), p. 319.

37. Louis Berkhof, *Systematic Theology* (London: The Banner of Truth Trust, 1949), p. 58.

38. Strong, *Systematic Theology*, p. 257.

39. David Jon Hill, "Why is God the Father Called a Father?" *Tomorrow's World* (September, 1970), p. 28.

40. B. McDowell, "Is the Holy Spirit a Person?" *Tomorrow's World* (September, 1970), pp. 31, 32.

41. Garner Ted Armstrong, "Do You Have an Immortal Soul?" Reprint No. 290, Ambassador College Press, 1971), p. 7.

42. Ibid., p. 8.

43. Edmond Gruss, *Apostles of Denial* (Philadelphia: The Presbyterian and Reformed Publishing Co., 1970), p. 157.

44. Loraine Boettner, *Immortality* (Philadelphia: The Presbyterian and Reformed Publishing Co., 1969), p. 123.

45. G. C. Berkouwer, *Man: The Image of God* (Grand Rapids: Wm. B. Eerdmans Publishing Co., 1962), p. 243.

46. Armstrong, "Do You Have an Immortal Soul?" p. 8.

47. Berkhof, *Systematic Theology*, p. 56.

48. Boettner, *Immortality*, p. 123.

49. Berkhof, *Systematic Theology*, p. 205.

50. Herbert W. Armstrong, *Lazarus and the Rich Man* (Pasadena: The Radio Church of God, 1953), p. 6.

51. Herbert W. Armstrong, *Just What Do You Mean . . . Born Again?* (Pasadena: Ambassador College Press, 1972), p. 27.

52. Walter Martin, *The Truth About Seventh-day Adventism* (Grand Rapids: Zondervan Publishing House, 1960), p. 122.

53. Merrill C. Tenney, *John: The Gospel of Belief* (Grand Rapids: Wm. B. Eerdmans Publishing Co., 1960), p. 122.

54. Ibid., p. 91.

55. Herbert W. Armstrong, ed. *Ambassador College Correspondence Course*, Lesson 5 (Pasadena: Ambassador College Press, 1972), p. 9.

56. Armstrong, "Do You Have an Immortal Soul?" p. 7.

57. D. M. Canright, *Seventh-day Adventism Renounced* (New York: Fleming H. Revell, 1889), pp. 401, 402.

58. Norman Douty, *Another Look at Seventh-day Adventism* (Grand Rapids: Baker Book House, 1962), p. 37.

59. Anthony Hoekema, *The Four Major Cults* (Grand Rapids: Wm. B. Eerdmans Publishing Co., 1963), p. 347. (Hereinafter referred to as *Major Cults*.)

60. Ibid., pp. 347, 348.

61. Herbert W. Armstrong, *The Book of Revelation Unveiled At Last!* (Pasadena: The Radio Church of God, 1959), p. 14.

62. See the following sources: Douty, pp. 36-41; Gruss, pp. 157 ff.; Martin, pp. 122 ff.; Hoekema, pp. 345 ff.; Boettner, pp. 78 ff.

63. Armstrong, *Correspondence Course*, Lesson 5, p. 9.

64. Ibid.

65. Hoekema, *Major Cults*, p. 349.

66. Gruss, *Apostles of Denial*, p. 159.

67. Hoekema, *Major Cults*, p. 350.

68. Armstrong, *Correspondence Course*, Lesson 5, p. 10.

69. This position was confirmed in an interview with Mr. Les Stocker of Ambassador College, Pasadena, Calif., January, 1973. The position is that God, like angels, is confined to one area at a time, but the Holy Spirit emanates from God and thus God is omnipresent.

70. Armstrong, *Correspondence Course*, Lesson 5, p. 10.

71. Ibid., p. 11.

72. Ibid., p. 10.

73. Berkhof, *Systematic Theology*, pp. 204, 205. See also Gordon H. Clark, "The Image of God in Man," *Journal of the Evangelical Theological Society*, XII, (Fall, 1969), p. 216. Clark concludes that the body could be included only in the sense that it is controlled by the spirit.

74. H. W. Armstrong, *Correspondence Course*, Lesson 5, pp. 9, 10.

75. G. T. Armstrong, "Do You Have an Immortal Soul?" p. 2.

76. Boettner, *Immortality*, pp. 123, 124.

77. Robert W. Landis, *The Immortality of the Soul* (New York: Carlton and Lanahan, 1868), pp. 120-122.

78. H. W. Armstrong, *Correspondence Course*, Lesson 6, p. 6.

79. William Dankenbring, "What is This Place Called Hell?" *Tomorrow's World* (July, 1970), p. 16.

80. Gruss, *Apostles of Denial*, p. 162.

81. Boettner, *Immortality*, p. 101.

82. Douty, *Another Look at Seventh-day Adventism*, p. 144.

83. Boettner, *Immortality*, p. 112.

84. Ambassador College Personal Correspondence Department, "Why Did Paul Want to Depart and Be With Christ?"

85. Hoekema, *Major Cults*, p. 357.

86. Charles Hodge, *Commentary on the Second Epistle to the Corinthians* (Grand Rapids: Wm. B. Eerdmans Publishing Co., n.d.), p. 110.

87. Ibid., p. 123.

88. Ambassador College Personal Correspondence Department, "Why Did Paul Want to Depart and Be With Christ?"

89. Martin, *The Truth About Seventh-day Adventism*, p. 124.

90. Armstrong, *Lazarus and the Rich Man*, pp. 4-10.

91. Ibid., p. 8.

92. Hoekema, *Major Cults*, p. 358.

93. G. T. Armstrong, "Will You Get to Heaven?" *Tomorrow's World* (July, 1970), p. 12.

94. Boettner, *Immortality*, pp. 113, 114.

95. Armstrong, *Correspondence Course*, Lexxon 6, pp. 12, 14.

96. Dankenbring, "What is This Place Called Hell?" p. 18.

97. Boettner, *Immortality*, p. 121.

98. Hoekema, *Major Cults*, pp. 361, 362.

99. Joachim Jeremias, "γέενα," *Theological Dictionary of the New Testament*, ed. by G. Kittel, trans. by G. Bromily, Vol. 1 (Grand Rapids: Wm. B. Eerdmans Publishing Co., 1965), p. 657.

100. Ibid., p. 658.

101. Arndt, W. F. and Gingrich, F. W. *A Greek-English Lexicon of the New Testament*, 4th ed. (Chicago: The University of Chicago Press, 1952), p. 441.

102. Ibid., p. 566.

103. Edmond Hiebert, *The Thessalonian Epistles* (Chicago: Moody Press, 1971), p. 213.

104. Hill, "Why is God the Father Called a Father?" *Tomorrow's World* (September, 1970), p. 27.

105. For a good treatment of this issue, see G. C. Berkouwer, *The Person of Christ* (Grand Rapids: Wm. B. Eerdmans Publishing Company, 1966), pp. 185-189.

106. Alva J. McClain, "The Doctrine of the Kenosis in Philippians 2:5-8," *Grace Journal*, VIII, No. 2 (1967), p. 10.

107. John F. Walvoord, *Jesus Christ Our Lord* (Chicago: Moody Press, 1969), p. 147.

108. See Berkouwer, *The Person of Christ*, pp. 239-267; Walvoord, *Jesus Christ Our Lord*, pp. 145-152; and L. Boettner, *The Person of Christ*, (Grand Rapids: Wm. B. Eerdmans Publishing Co., 1943), pp. 123 ff.

109. H. W. Armstrong, "Why Christ Died—and Rose Again!" *Tomorrow's World* (March, 1970), p. 5.

110. McClain, "The Doctrine of the Kenosis in Philippians 2:5-8," p. 9.

111. Wilbur Smith, *Therefore Stand* (Boston: W. A. Wilde Co., 1946), pp. 406-08; W. J. Sparrow-Simpson, *Our Lord's Resurrection* (Grand Rapids: Zondervan Publishing House, 1964), pp. 159-75; Walvoord, *Jesus Christ our Lord*, pp. 200-05.

112. H. W. Armstrong, *Just What Do You Mean . . . Born Again?* (Pasadena: Ambassador College Press, 1962), p. 7.

113. Ibid.

114. Buchsel, "γεννάω," *Theological Dictionary of the New Testament*, ed. by G. Kittel, trans. by G. Bromiley, Vol. 1 (Grand Rapids: Wm. B. Eerdmans Publishing Co., 1965), pp. 665-675.

115. Meredith, *The Ten Commandments*, p. 17.

Chapter 5

1. David Jon Hill, "Twelve Rules for Bible Study," *The Plain Truth* (September, 1964), pp. 12 ff.

2. Ibid., p. 13.

3. R. L. Kuhn, "How to Understand Prophecy," *Tomorrow's World* (January, 1971), p. 41.

4. Roderick Meredith, "The True Church—Where is It?" *The Plain Truth* (March, 1963), p. 45.

5. Richard Marson, *The Marson Report Concerning Herbert W. Armstrong* (Seattle: The Ashley-Calvin Press, 1970), p. 7.

6. Ibid., p. 10.

7. Roger Chambers, *The Plain Truth About Armstrongism* (Grand Rapids: Baker Book House, 1972), p. 82.

8. H. W. Armstrong, *The Plain Truth About Christmas* (Pasadena: Ambassador College Press, 1970), p. 18.

9. Anthony Hoekema, *The Four Major Cults* (Grand Rapids: Wm. B. Eerdmans Publishing Co., 1970), p. 251.

10. Paul Wilson, *The Armstrong Heresy* (Denver, Colorado: Wilson Foundation, n.d.), p. 6.

11. H. W. Armstrong, *The United States and British Commonwealth in Prophecy* (Pasadena: Ambassador College Press, 1967), pp. 113-15.

12. Ibid., p. 30.

13. H. W. Armstrong, *The Book of Revelation Unveiled At Last!* (Pasadena: The Radio Church of God, 1959), p. 13.

14. Armstrong, *The United States and British Commonwealth in Prophecy*, pp. 132, 134.

15. David Jeremiah, "The Principle of Double Fulfillment," *Grace Journal*, Vol. 13, No. 2 (Spring, 1972), p. 18.

16. Armstrong, *Revelation Unveiled At Last!* p. 14.

17. Armstrong, *The United States and British Commonwealth in Prophecy,* p. 103.

Conclusion

1. Roderick Meredith, *The Ten Commandments* (Pasadena: Ambassador College Press, 1968), p. 29.

Bibliography

Armstrongism: Books and Booklets

Ambassador College Correspondence Course. Lessons 1–11. Pasadena: Ambassador College Press, 1972.

Ambassador College Research Department. *Famine: Can We Survive?* Pasadena: Ambassador College Press, 1969.

Armstrong, Herbert W. *All About Water Baptism.* Pasadena: Ambassador College Press, 1972.

—————. *The Autobiography of Herbert W. Armstrong.* Vol. 1. Pasadena: Ambassador College Press, 1967.

—————. *The Book of Revelation—Unveiled At Last!* Pasadena: Radio Church of God, 1959.

—————. *Does God Exist?* Pasadena: Ambassador College Press, 1957.

—————. *Just What Do You Mean . . . Born Again?* Pasadena: Ambassador College Press, 1972.

—————. *Just What Do You Mean . . . Kingdom of God?* Pasadena: Ambassador College Press, 1962.

—————. *The Key to the Book of Revelation.* Pasadena: Ambassador College Press, 1952.

—————. *The Plain Truth About Christmas.* Pasadena: Ambassador College Press, 1970.

—————. *The Plain Truth About Easter.* Pasadena: Ambassador College Press, 1957.

—————. *The Resurrection Was Not on Sunday!* Pasadena: Ambassador College Press, 1952.

—————. *The United States and British Commonwealth in Prophecy.* Pasadena: Ambassador College Press, 1967.

—————. *What is Faith?* Pasadena: Ambassador College Press, 1952.

—————. *Which Day is the Christian Sabbath?* Pasadena: Ambassador College Press, 1971.

—————. *Why Were You Born?* Pasadena: Ambassador College Press, 1957.

—————. *1975 in Prophecy.* Pasadena: Ambassador College Press, 1952.

Armstrong, Garner Ted, and Armstrong, Herbert W. *The Wonderful World Tomorrow*. Pasadena: Ambassador College Press, 1966.

Hoeh, Herman L. *A True History of the True Church*. Pasadena: Ambassador College Press, 1959.

Meredith, Roderick C. *The Ten Commandments*. Pasadena: Ambassador College Press, 1968.

This is Ambassador College. Pasadena: Ambassador College Press, 1969.

This is the Worldwide Church of God. Pasadena: Ambassador College Press, 1972.

Armstrongism: Key Magazine Articles

Armstrong, Garner Ted. "Are You Under the Law?" *Tomorrow's World*, January 1971, pp. 6 ff.

_____ . "Will You Get to Heaven?" *Tomorrow's World*, July 1970, pp. 9-13.

Armstrong, Herbert W. "Millions Do Not Know What Christ Really Was!" *The Plain Truth*, November 1963, pp. 9-12.

_____ . "The 19 Year Time Cycles." *Tomorrow's World*, February 1972, pp. 1 ff.

_____ . "Was Jesus Christ Born Again?" *The Plain Truth*, February 1963, pp. 7 ff.

_____ . "What Do You Mean . . . 'The Unpardonable Sin'?" *Tomorrow's World*, July 1971, pp. 1 ff.

_____ . "Why Christ Died and Rose Again!" *Tomorrow's World*, March 1970, pp. 5-8.

_____ . "Why Must Men Suffer?" *Tomorrow's World*, December 1969, pp. 5 ff.

Dankenbring, William F. "What is This Place Called Hell?" *Tomorrow's World*, July 1970, pp. 14-18.

Geis, George. "The God Family: Open or Closed?" *Tomorrow's World*, September 1970, p. 30.

Grabbe, J. Orlin. "Only One God is God!" *Tomorrow's World*, March 1972, pp. 19-22.

Hill, David Jon. "There is a Real Hell Fire!" *The Plain Truth*, January 1963, pp. 11-14.

_____ . "Why is God the Father Called a Father?" *Tomorrow's World*, September 1970, pp. 24-28.

Hill, David Jon, and Kuhn, Robert L. "Why Does God Hide Himself?" *Tomorrow's World*, December 1969, pp. 9 ff.

Hoeh, Herman L. "Where Did Jesus Command You to Observe Sunday?" *The Plain Truth*, December 1962, pp. 21-29.

Kuhn, Robert L. "What It Means to be Equal With God?" *Tomorrow's World*, April 1971, pp. 43-45.

McCullough, Leslie. "Just What Do You Mean—Repentance?" *Tomorrow's World*, December 1971, pp. 29 ff.

McDowell, B. "Is the Holy Spirit a Person?" *Tomorrow's World*, September 1970, p. 31.

Portune, Albert J. "Will There Be a Secret Rapture?" *The Plain Truth*, February 1963, pp. 31 ff.

Wiedenheft, Richard A. "Why Christ Spoke in Parables," *Tomorrow's World*, July 1971, p. 15.

Works Dealing With Armstrongism

Chambers, Roger R. *The Plain Truth About Armstrongism*. Grand Rapids: Baker Book House, 1972.

DeLoach, Charles F. *The Armstrong Error*. Plainfield, New Jersey: Logos International, 1971.

Lowe, Harry. *Radio Church of God*. Mountain View, California: Pacific Press Publishing Association, 1970.

Marson, Richard A. *The Marson Report Concerning Herbert W. Armstrong*. Seattle: The Ashley-Calvin Press, 1970.

Martin, Walter R. *Herbert W. Armstrong and the Radio Church of God*. Minneapolis: Bethany Fellowship, Inc., 1968.

Trefry, Robert Arthur. "The Theology of Herbert W. & Garner T. Armstrong." Unpublished Th.M. thesis, Dallas Theological Seminary, Dallas, Texas, 1968, pp. iii+64.

Wilson, Paul. *The Armstrong Heresy*. Denver: Wilson Foundation, n.d.

General Works

Abbott-Smith, G. A. *A Manual Lexicon of the New Testament*. 3rd ed. Edinburgh: T. & T. Clark, 1960.

Arndt, W. F. and Gingrich, F. W. *A Greek-English Lexicon of the New Testament*. 4th ed. Chicago: University of Chicago Press, 1952.

Allen, J. H. *Judah's Sceptre and Joseph's Birthright*. 17th ed. Boston: A. A. Beauchamp, 1943.

Baron, David. *The History of the Ten 'Lost' Tribes*. 3rd ed. London: Morgan & Scott Ld., 1915.

Barton, George A. *Archaeology and the Bible*. Philadelphia: American Sunday School Union, 1917.

Berkhof, Louis. *Systematic Theology*. London: The Banner of Truth Trust, 1949.

Berkouwer, G. C. *Man: The Image of God*. Grand Rapids: Wm. B. Eerdmans Publishing Co., 1962.

——————. *The Person of Christ*. Grand Rapids: Wm. B. Eerdmans Publishing Co., 1966.

Boettner, Loraine. *Immortality*. Philadelphia: The Presbyterian and Reformed Publishing Co., 1969.

——————. *The Person of Christ*. Grand Rapids: Wm. B. Eerdmans Publishing Co., 1943.

Branson, Wm. H. *Drama of the Ages*. Nashville: Southern Publishing Association, 1953.

Bright, John. *A History of Israel*. Philadelphia: The Westminster Press, 1959.

Canright, D. M. *Seventh-day Adventism Renounced.* 2nd ed. Chicago: Fleming H. Revell, 1889.

Chafer, L. S. *Salvation.* Grand Rapids: Zondervan Publishing House, 1971.

Cooper, David L. *Man: His Creation, Fall, Redemption and Glorification.* Los Angeles: Biblical Research Society, 1948.

Darms, Anton. *The Delusion of British Israelism.* New York: Publication Office "Our Hope," n.d.

Douty, Norman. *Another Look at Seventh-day Adventism.* Grand Rapids: Baker Book House, 1962.

Duff-Forbes, Lawrence. *The Baleful Bubble of "British-Israelism."* Los Angeles: Marathon Press, 1961.

Finegan, Jack. *Light From the Ancient Past.* Princeton, New Jersey: Princeton University Press, 1946.

Froom, LeRoy Edwin. *The Conditionalist Faith of Our Fathers.* 2 vols. Washington, D. C.: The Review and Herald Publishing Co., 1966.

Gerstner, John H. *The Theology of the Major Sects.* Grand Rapids: Baker Book House, 1960.

Girdlestone, Robert B. *Synonyms of the Old Testament.* Grand Rapids, Wm. B. Eerdmans Publishing Co., 1956.

Gruss, Edmond C. *Apostles of Denial.* Philadelphia: The Presbyterian and Reformed Publishing Co., 1970.

Hiebert, D. Edmond. *The Thessalonian Epistles.* Chicago: Moody Press, 1971.

Hodge, Charles. *Commentary on the Second Epistle to the Corinthians.* Grand Rapids: Wm. B. Eerdmans Publishing Co., n.d.

Hoekema, Anthony A. *The Four Major Cults.* Grand Rapids: Wm. B. Eerdmans Publishing Co., 1963.

Jewish Encyclopedia. Vol. VII. New York: Funk and Wagnalls Corp., 1904.

Irvine, William C., ed. *Heresies Exposed.* New York: Loizeaux Bros., 1945.

Keil, C. F. *Biblical Commentary on the Old Testament: The Prophecies of Jeremiah.* 2 vols. Translated by James Kennedy. Edinburgh: T. & T. Clark, 1874.

Kittel, Gerhard, ed. *Theological Dictionary of the New Testament.* 8 vols. Translated and edited by Geoffrey W. Bromiley. Grand Rapids: Wm. B. Eerdmans Publishing Co., 1963.

Lamb, W. *Anglo-Israelism: True or False?* Sydney, Australia: St. Andrews Place, 1935.

Landis, Robert W. *The Immortality of the Soul.* New York: Carlton and Lanahan, 1868.

Let God Be True. Brooklyn: Watchtower Bible and Tract Society, Inc., 1952.

Leupold, H. C. *Exposition of Genesis.* 2 vols. Grand Rapids: Baker Book House, 1970.

Lewis, Gordon R. *Confronting the Cults.* Philadelphia: The Presbyterian and Reformed Publishing Company, 1966.

Lightfoot, J. B. *The Epistle of St. Paul to the Galatians.* Grand Rapids: Zondervan Publishing House, 1967.

Martin, Walter R. *The Kingdom of the Cults.* Minneapolis: Bethany Fellowship, Inc., 1968.

——————. *The Rise of the Cults.* Grand Rapids: Zondervan Publishing House, 1955.

——————. *The Truth About Seventh-day Adventism.* Grand Rapids: Zondervan Publishing House, 1960.

McClain, Alva J. *The Greatness of the Kingdom.* Chicago: Moody Press, 1968.

Mitchell, David. *Seventh-day Adventists.* New York: Vantage Press, Inc. 1958.

Muller, Jac. J. *The Epistles of Paul to the Philippians and to Philemon.* Grand Rapids: Wm. B. Eerdmans Publishing Co., 1970.

Murray, John. *The Epistle to the Romans.* Vol. 1. Grand Rapids: Wm. B. Eerdmans Publishing Co., 1959.

Pache, Rene. *The Person and Work of the Holy Spirit.* Chicago: Moody Press, 1960.

Pentecost, J. Dwight. *Things to Come.* Grand Rapids: Dunham Publishing Co., 1964.

Perowne, J. J. Stewart. *The Book of Psalms.* London: George Bell and Sons, 1898.

Pfeiffer, Charles F. *The Divided Kingdom.* Grand Rapids: Baker Book House, 1967.

Ramm, Bernard. *Protestant Biblical Interpretation.* Boston: W. A. Wilde Co., 1956.

——————. *A Handbook of Contemporary Theology.* Grand Rapids: Wm. B. Eerdmans Publishing Co., 1966.

Rose, George L. *Real Israel Versus Anglo-Israelism.* 2nd ed. Glendale, California: Rose Publishing Co., 1942.

Roy, Ralph L. *Apostles of Discord.* Boston: The Beacon Press, 1953.

Sanday, Wm. and Headlam, Arthur. *A Critical and Exegetical Commentary on the Epistle to the Romans.* 5th ed. Edinburgh: T. & T. Clark, 1964.

Sanders, J. Oswald. *Heresies and Cults.* London: Marshall, Morgan and Scott, 1962.

Saucy, Robert L. *The Church in God's Program.* Chicago: Moody Press, 1972.

Sauer, Erich. *The Triumph of the Crucified.* Grand Rapids: Wm. B. Eerdmans Publishing Co., 1963.

Smith, Joseph Fielding, ed. *Teachings of the Prophet Joseph Smith.* Salt Lake City: Deseret Book Co., 1970.

Smith, Wilbur. *Therefore Stand.* Boston: W. A. Wilde Co., 1946.

Sparrow-Simpson, J. W. *Our Lord's Resurrection.* Grand Rapids: Zondervan Publishing House, 1964.

Stifler, James M. *The Epistle to the Romans.* Chicago: Moody Press, 1960.

Strong, Augustus H. *Systematic Theology.* Old Tappen, New Jersey: Fleming H. Revell Co., 1969.

Talmage, James E. *A Study of the Articles of Faith.* 17th ed. Salt Lake City: The Church of Jesus Christ of Latter-day Saints, 1937.

Tenney, Merrill C. *John: The Gospel of Belief.* Grand Rapids: Wm. B. Eerdmans Publishing Co., 1965.

Trench, Richard. *Synonyms of the New Testament.* New York: Redfield, 1854.

Van Baalen, J. Karel. *The Chaos of the Cults.* Grand Rapids: Wm. B. Eerdmans Publishing Co., 1956.

Vine, W. E. *The Epistles of John.* Grand Rapids: Zondervan Publishing House, n.d.

Vine, W. E. *An Expository Dictionary of New Testament Words.* London Oliphants Ltd., 1963.

Walvoord, John F. *Jesus Christ Our Lord.* Chicago: Moody Press, 1969.

_____. *The Millennial Kingdom.* Findlay, Ohio: Dunham Publishing Co., 1963.

Whitcomb, John C. *Solomon to the Exile.* Winona Lake, Indiana: B.M.H. Books, 1971.

Wood, Leon. *A Survey of Israel's History.* Grand Rapids: Zondervan Publishing House, 1971.

Periodicals

Aldrich, Roy L. "Has the Mosaic Law Been Abolished?" *Bibliotheca Sacra,* Vol. 116 (October 1959), 322-35.

Campbell, Roger. "Pertinent Answers to Armstrongism." *The King's Business,* September 1963, pp. 14, 15.

Caneday, Herbert V. "What Does Herbert Armstrong Preach?" *The King's Business,* December 1959, pp. 26, 27.

Clark, Gordon H. "The Image of God in Man." *Journal of the Evangelical Theological Society,* XII (Fall, 1969), pp. 215-22.

Cook, W. Robert. "Hamartiological Problems in First John." *Bibliotheca Sacra,* Vol. 123 (July,1966), 249-60.

"Domestic Relations: Alienated by Radio." *Time,* March 22, 1968, pp. 52, 53.

Ellison, H. L. "The Prophecy of Jeremiah." *The Evangelical Quarterly,* XXXIX (January 1967), pp. 40-46.

Feinberg, Charles. "The Image of God." *Bibliotheca Sacra,* Vol. 129 (July 1972), 235-46.

Haines, A. B. "Colleges Re-educate for Christ's Return." *The Christian Century,* LXXXVI (February 19, 1969), p. 264.

Hopkins, Joseph Martin. "Herbert W. Armstrong." *Christianity Today,* December 17, 1971, pp. 6-9.

Howie, Carl G. "British Israelism and Pyramidology." *Interpretation,* XI (July 1957), 307-23.

Hoyt, Herman A. "The Explanation of the New Birth." *Grace Journal,* Vol. 8 (Spring, 1967), 14-21.

Jeremiah, David. "The Principle of Double Fulfillment in Interpreting Prophecy." *Grace Journal,* Vol. 13 (Spring, 1972), 13-29.

Martin, William C. "The God-Hucksters of Radio." *The Atlantic Monthly,* June 1970, pp. 51-57.

McClain, Alva J. "The Doctrine of the Kenosis in Philippians 2:5-8." *Grace Journal,* Vol. 8 (Spring, 1967), 3-13.

Metzger, Bruce. "The Jehovah's Witnesses and Jesus Christ." *Theology Today,* X (April 1953), 65-85.

Robinson, Haddon W. "The Impact of Religious Radio and Television Programs on American Life." *Bibliotheca Sacra,* Vol. 123 (April 1966), 124-35.

Ryrie, Charles C. "The End of the Law." *Bibliotheca Sacra,* Vol. 124 (July 1967), 239-47.

Tarr, Leslie K. "Herbert W. Armstrong: Does He Really Have the 'Plain Truth'?" *Moody Monthly,* September 1972, pp. 24-27.

Unger, Merrill F. "The Significance of the Sabbath." *Bibliotheca Sacra,* Vol. 123 (January 1966), 53-59.

"The Vice-President is Missing." *Christianity Today,* April 14, 1972, p. 39.

Newspaper Articles

Barber, Carter. "Vice-Chancellor Armstrong Said on Leave of Absence." *Pasadena Star News,* March 18, 1972.

Dart, John. "Preacher Attacks 'Evils' of Religious Sects." *Los Angeles Times,* July 29, 1972, 1. 25.

Geiger, Peter. "Church Cut Us Off From Family, Friends." *Akron (Ohio) Beacon Journal,* October 11, 1970, A. 6.

Hansen, Earl. "Where Are You, Garner Ted?" *Seattle Post-Intelligencer,* March 25, 1972, A. 8.

Kinsolving, Lester. "A Gold Mine in Pasadena." *Seattle Post-Intelligencer,* March 12, 1972.

"Preacher Will Return to T.V." *Los Angeles Times,* June 3, 1972, 1. 30.